# LONGMAN
# SCIENCE

## EARTH

Roland Scal

PEARSON
Longman

**Longman Science: Earth**

Pearson Education, 10 Bank Street, White Plains, NY 10606 USA

**Staff credits:** The people who made up the **Longman Science: Earth** team,
representing editorial, production, design, manufacturing, and marketing
are John Ade, Margaret Antonini, Rhea Banker, Gina DiLillo, Ed Lamprich,
Tara Maceyak, Liza Pleva, Barbara Sabella, Tania Saiz-Sousa, Susan Saslow,
and Patricia Wosczyk.
**Text design and composition:** The Quarasan Group, Inc.
**Text font:** 12.5/16 Minion Regular
**Photo and illustration credits:** See page 155.

**Library of Congress Cataloging-in-Publication Data**
Scal, Roland.
    Longman Science: Earth / Contributor: Scal, Roland.
    p. cm.
    Includes index.
    ISBN-13: 978-0-13-267940-4
    ISBN-10: 0-13-267940-X
    1. Science—Study and teaching (Secondary)
      I. Pearson Education, Inc.
    Q181.L824 2011
    500—dc22

ISBN-13: 978-0-13-267940-4
ISBN-10: 0-13-267940-X

**PEARSON LONGMAN** ON THE **WEB**

**Pearsonlongman.com** offers online
resources for teachers and students. Access our
Companion Websites, our online catalog, and
our local offices around the world.

Visit us at **www.pearsonlongman.com.**

Printed in the United States of America
1 2 3 4 5 6 7 8 9 10—V011—15 14 13 12 11

# Contents

# Introduction

# Part 2 Planets and Stars

v

# What Is Science?

Science is the study of the natural world. It is the study of Earth and other planets. It is the study of the animals and plants on Earth. Science is the study of every living and nonliving thing around us.

Scientists study our world. They ask questions and look for answers. Scientists watch carefully. Then they try to understand.

Scientists study Earth and other planets. ▼

▲ Scientists study animals, like this koala. They also study plants, like this tree.

Scientists study different kinds of matter and energy. ▶

For more practice, go to page 29.

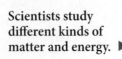

# The Sciences

Scientists study different kinds of sciences. In this book you'll learn about life science, Earth science, and physical science.

## Earth Science

Earth science is the study of the Earth and outer space. It is the study of the land, water, and air on the Earth. It is the study of all the materials that make up the Earth and everything else in the universe. Earth science is the study of the sun you see in the day. It is the study of the stars you see at night. It is also the study of other planets far away from Earth.

▲ Water, air, land, and living things make up Earth's environment.

This is the planet Saturn.
It is far away from Earth. ▼

▲ Hot liquid rock, called lava, comes out of volcanoes when they erupt.

# Life Science

Life science is the study of living things on the Earth. Animals are living things. Plants are also living things.

▲ Some scientists study only frogs.

▲ This scientist studies plants.

▲ Some scientists study only plants and animals that live underwater.

# Physical Science

Physical science is the study of matter. Air is matter. Rocks are matter. And water is matter. They are nonliving matter. Physical scientists study mostly nonliving matter.

Physical science is also the study of energy. Electricity is an example of energy. Sound and light are also **types** of energy.

---

**types:** kinds

▲ Electricity is a type of energy. Lightning is electricity.

◀ The boy in this photograph is living matter. Everything else is nonliving matter.

**Before You Go On**

1. What is the environment?
2. What are some examples of matter?
3. What are some examples of energy?

For more practice, go to pages 30–32.

# Meet a Scientist

Paula Messina is a scientist and a teacher. She studies the Earth's surface. She studied the rocks in Death Valley National Park, California. Some of the rocks were large boulders, as heavy as five adults, and others were smaller than eggs. Messina noticed something very unusual.

She **observed** trails that led to the rocks. The trails made it seem as though the rocks had moved there. Messina wanted to understand how the rocks had moved, carving trails as they went. No one had ever seen the rocks moving.

---

**observed:** studied by looking at

**Earth scientist and teacher Paula Messina on the salt flats in Death Valley National Park ▶**

▲ Two rocks and their trails on the dry soil of Racetrack Playa

**Illustration of Racetrack Playa in its surroundings: the black lines show a 1996 mapping of the rock trails. The large arrows show the direction of the winds that push the rocks. ▶**

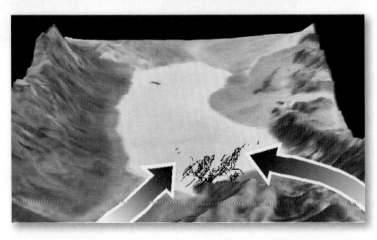

Since 1996, Messina has gone to Racetrack Playa many times to make maps of the rocks and trails. From her maps, Messina can see where the rocks have moved. But still, even after years of research, she has never seen the rocks move!

◄ Several of the sliding rocks with their trails. The trail of the closest rock shows how it changed direction as it moved.

The white area in the middle is Racetrack Playa. ▶

# The Scientific Method

How do scientists find out information about the world? How do they understand the information? How do they show others their ideas are correct?

Scientists use the scientific method. This is how scientists find out about the world. Five important steps of the scientific method are (1) asking questions, (2) making a **hypothesis**, (3) testing the hypothesis, (4) observing, and (5) **drawing conclusions**.

---

**hypothesis:** a guess; an idea
**drawing conclusions:** deciding about something

◀ Scientists look at things carefully.

Scientists measure things. This scientist is using beakers to make measurements. ▼

# Asking Questions

Scientists ask questions about the world. They begin with things they know. They ask questions about things they don't know.

For example, you have questions about plants. You know seeds grow into plants. But you don't know how. You ask, "What is something that seeds need to grow?"

▼ This plant grew from a seed.

▲ Scientists look at the world and ask questions.

▼ These are seeds.

## Before You Go On

1. How do scientists show others their ideas are correct?
2. What are the five steps of the scientific method?
3. What's an example of asking questions?

# Making a Hypothesis

After asking a question, scientists try to guess the answer. This is called making a hypothesis.

You asked, "What is something that seeds need to grow?" You think about what you already know about plants. Then you make a guess. You think, "The seeds need water to grow." This is your hypothesis.

▲ You get a paper towel, a glass jar, and some beans.

▲ You put a bean, paper towel, and water in the jar. You put a bean and dry paper towel in another jar.

# Testing the Hypothesis

After scientists make a hypothesis, they test it. They find out if their idea is correct. Doing an experiment is a good way to test a hypothesis.

To test your hypothesis about seeds, you think of an experiment. You know beans are big seeds. You have some beans in the kitchen. You put paper towels and beans into two jars. Then you add water to one of the jars.

# Observing

Scientists observe, or look, listen, touch, and think. Observing is an important part of the scientific method.

During your bean experiment, you look at the two jars every day. You observe that the bean in the jar with water takes in water and gets bigger. Then you observe this bean growing into a plant. You also see that the bean in the jar with no water does not grow into a plant.

◀ The bean in the jar with water gets bigger and begins to grow.

It is changing into a plant. ▶

## Before You Go On

1. What do scientists do after they make a hypothesis?
2. What's a good way to test a hypothesis?
3. How do scientists observe?

# Drawing Conclusions

After scientists observe, they decide if their hypothesis is correct. This is called drawing conclusions.

The bean experiment tested the hypothesis *seeds need water to grow*. You observed that the beans grew with water but not without water. The hypothesis is correct. Your conclusion is *seeds need water to grow*.

▲ This scientist is observing plants growing in pots.

▲ This plant is growing in water. Plants need water to grow.

You can ask more questions about the bean plant. Will the plant continue to grow? Will it be a healthy plant? Does it need something else to grow well?

A scientist continues to observe and ask questions. A scientist thinks of another hypothesis and tests it. Then he or she draws other conclusions. Using the scientific method helps us learn about the world.

## Scientific Method

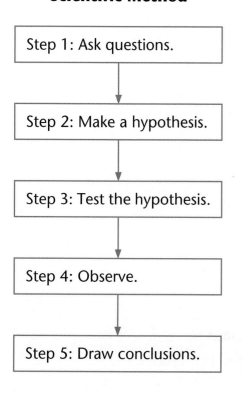

Step 1: Ask questions.

↓

Step 2: Make a hypothesis.

↓

Step 3: Test the hypothesis.

↓

Step 4: Observe.

↓

Step 5: Draw conclusions.

▲ This scientist is studying a flower.

### Before You Go On

1. What do scientists do after they observe?
2. What is the conclusion of the bean experiment?
3. What other questions can you ask about the bean plant?

For more practice, go to pages 33–34.

# Safety

Safety is very important in the science classroom. Always follow these basic safety rules. They will keep you and your classmates safe.

You will do an experiment to help you understand the scientific method. But first, learn these basic safety rules.

### Make Sure You Understand

Read experiment instructions carefully. Make sure you understand before you begin. Ask your teacher when you don't understand.

### Be Careful with Scissors

Always point scissors away from your body. When you carry scissors, point them down. Keep your fingers far away from scissor blades.

### Stay Away from Broken Glass

If glass breaks, tell your teacher. Don't pick it up yourself.

### Tell Your Teacher If You Hurt Yourself

If you cut or hurt yourself, tell your teacher right away.

## Clean Up Spills

Clean up any spills right away. Tell your teacher if anything spills on the floor.

## Be Careful with Electricity

Be careful with things that use electricity. Don't use electrical items near water. Make sure the cords are out of the way.

## Be Careful with Hot Things

Be careful with anything that is hot. Don't touch it until you know it is cool.

## Keep Things Clean

Keep the experiment area clean and neat. Always put things away after you finish an experiment.

### Before You Go On

1. Why do you follow safety rules?
2. What do you need to be careful with?
3. How do you carry scissors?

For more practice, go to pages 35–36.

# Practicing the Scientific Method

Practice using the scientific method as a class. Follow each step as you do the experiment on page 17.

1. **Ask questions.** Look at the pictures. **Sedimentary rocks** have layers of **sediment** of different colors and textures. How do the layers form?

2. **Make a hypothesis.** Think about what you already know about different kinds of rocks and what you have noticed about the layers. Guess how the layers form. Your guess is your hypothesis.

3. **Test the hypothesis.** Do the experiment on the next page. It will test your hypothesis.

---

**sedimentary rocks:** rocks formed by different kinds of sediment over time

**sediment:** particles, or small pieces, that break off rocks and other natural materials

# Experiment

## How do the layers of sedimentary rocks form?

### Purpose

To find one way sediments form layers

### Materials

soil from a local field (do not use commercial potting soil)

jars with straight sides and lids

water

plastic spoons or sticks

### What to Do

1. Fill the jars 1/3 of the way with loose dry soil. Break up chunks and discard large pebbles.

2. Fill the jar with water, put on the lid, and shake the mixture until well mixed. Look at the mixture.

3. Let the mixture settle overnight. It may take several hours for the water to clear.

### Draw Conclusions

What happened to the mixture? Does it look different from the way it looked after step 3? How? Why did this happen?

4. **Observe.** Look at the mixture. Write down what you see in your Experiment Log. Draw a picture of the mixture before and after your experiment. Show what is in the different layers of sediment and their colors.

5. **Draw conclusions.** What did you learn about how layers of sediment form? This is your conclusion. Talk about what you learned with your classmates.

# Experiment Log: How do the layers of sedimentary rocks form?

Follow the steps of the scientific method as you do your experiment.
Write notes about each step as the experiment progresses.

**Step 1: Ask questions.**

**Step 2: Make a hypothesis.**

Draw a picture here of the jar of soil and water after you shook it up.

**Step 3: Test your hypothesis.**

**Step 4: Observe.**

Draw a picture here of the jar of soil and water after it settled overnight.

**Step 5: Draw conclusions.**

# Science Tools

How hot is it? How fast is it? How big is it? How heavy is it? The tools on this page help scientists measure things. You will use some of these tools as you study science.

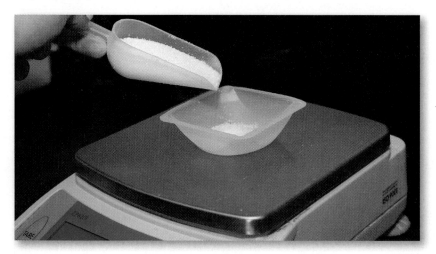

◀ A **balance** measures how heavy something is.

A **stopwatch** measures time. ▶

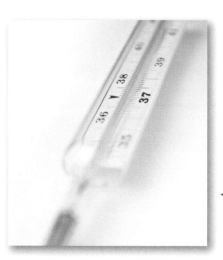

◀ A **thermometer** measures how hot or cold something is.

▲ A **ruler** measures distance. It helps us measure how long something is. This ruler shows both centimeters and inches. Scientists usually use centimeters.

How do you see something that is very small? How do you see a star far away in the sky? Scientists often use lenses made of glass. The tools on this page all have lenses.

▲ A **hand lens** lets us see small things close up.

▲ A **camera** lets us take pictures.

▲ A **telescope** helps us see distant stars.

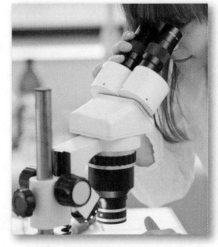

▲ A **microscope** lets us see very small things.

### Before You Go On

1. What tool measures how hot or cold something is?
2. What four tools have lenses?
3. Which tool lets us see things far away in the sky?

For more practice, go to pages 37–38.

# Visuals

After scientists learn information, they tell others about it. Scientists often use visuals to share information. These are some of the visuals you will study in this book.

| Sound | Volume in Decibels |
|-------|:---:|
| Shuttle taking off | 190 |
| Rock concert | 115 |
| Busy street | 70 |
| Classroom or office | 45 |
| Falling leaves | 10 |

▲ Chart

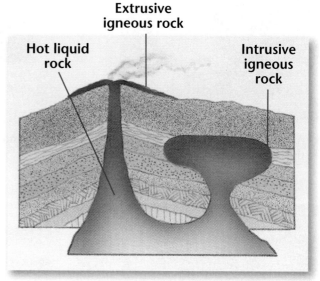

▲ Sectional diagram

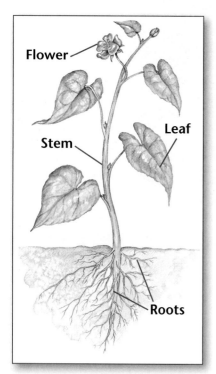

▲ Diagram

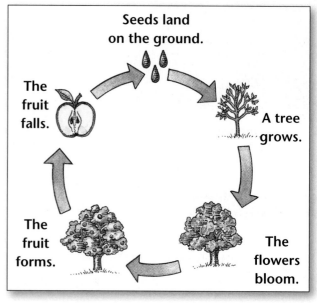

▲ Cycle diagram

# Birds

▲ Pie chart

▲ Illustration

▲ Photograph

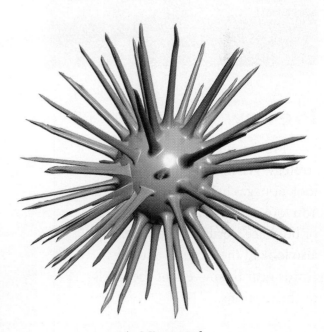

▲ Micrograph

## Before You Go On

1. What do scientists use visuals for?
2. Which visuals give information using words and numbers?
3. Which visuals use pictures?

For more practice, go to pages 39–40.

# Science Reading Strategies

In this book, you'll use science reading strategies. These strategies are special ways to look at and think about the text in your science book. These strategies will help you understand and remember what you read.

◀ Good readers use reading strategies.

## Preview

Previewing is a reading strategy. When you preview, you look at pages before you read them. You look at the headings—the big or boldface words on the page. You also look at the pictures and the words near them—either the labels or the captions.

Preview ▶

Headings

All of the Earth's rocks form in three ways. Rocks are grouped by how they form.

### Igneous Rock

Igneous rock forms when hot liquid rock cools and becomes hard. There are two kinds of igneous rock: extrusive and intrusive. Extrusive igneous rock forms, for instance, on the surface after a volcano erupts. The liquid rock cools and hardens above ground. Intrusive igneous rock cools and hardens underground. You can't see this kind of rock until the rock and soil that cover it are worn away.

**SCIENCE AT HOME**

**Pumice**

Pumice is an igneous rock. Pumice has a rough texture—it feels rough. It is used in many beauty products. People rub pumice on their feet. This helps make the skin smooth.

▲ A woman rubs her foot with pumice.

Pictures

Hot liquid rock from a volcano cools. It becomes extrusive igneous rock. ▼

▲ This intrusive igneous rock was once underground. The rock and soil that once covered it have worn away.

# Predict

Another good reading strategy is predicting. To predict means to guess what a text is about. While you preview, predict what you will learn about.

I will learn about igneous rock—where it comes from and some of its uses.

All of the Earth's rocks form in three ways. Rocks are grouped by how they form.

## Igneous Rock

Igneous rock forms when hot liquid rock cools and becomes hard. There are two kinds of igneous rock: extrusive and intrusive. Extrusive igneous rock forms, for instance, on the surface after a volcano erupts. The liquid rock cools and hardens above ground. Intrusive igneous rock cools and hardens underground. You can't see this kind of rock until the rock and soil that cover it are worn away.

▲ This intrusive igneous rock was once underground. The rock and soil that once covered it have worn away.

Hot liquid rock from a volcano cools. It becomes extrusive igneous rock. ▼

**SCIENCE AT HOME**

**Pumice**

Pumice is an igneous rock. Pumice has a rough texture—it feels rough. It is used in many beauty products. People rub pumice on their feet. This helps make the skin smooth.

▲ A woman rubs her foot with pumice.

▲ Predict

▲ Most people preview and predict when they first look at a magazine.

## Before You Go On

1. How are science reading strategies helpful?

2. How do you preview?

3. What does *predict* mean?

## Check Your Understanding

Complete each sentence with the correct word or phrase.

1. _____ science is the study of the Earth.
   **a.** Physical  **b.** Life  **c.** Earth

2. _____ science is the study of living things.
   **a.** Earth  **b.** Life  **c.** Physical

3. _____ science is the study of matter and energy.
   **a.** Life  **b.** Physical  **c.** Earth

4. Asking questions and making a hypothesis are steps in the _____.
   **a.** visuals  **b.** science tools  **c.** scientific method

5. Doing an experiment is a good way to test a _____.
   **a.** hypothesis  **b.** conclusion  **c.** safety rule

6. Scientists _____ by watching very carefully.
   **a.** guess  **b.** observe  **c.** ask

7. After an experiment, scientists draw _____.
   **a.** conclusions  **b.** questions  **c.** safety rules

8. A thermometer, a telescope, and a balance are science _____.
   **a.** visuals  **b.** tools  **c.** strategies

9. A diagram, a pie chart, and a micrograph are _____.
   **a.** tools  **b.** strategies  **c.** visuals

10. Previewing and predicting are reading _____.
    **a.** strategies  **b.** tools  **c.** visuals

# Apply Science Skills

## Science Reading Strategy: **Preview and Predict**

As a class, preview pages 54–55. As you preview, predict. Tell your teacher what you will learn about.

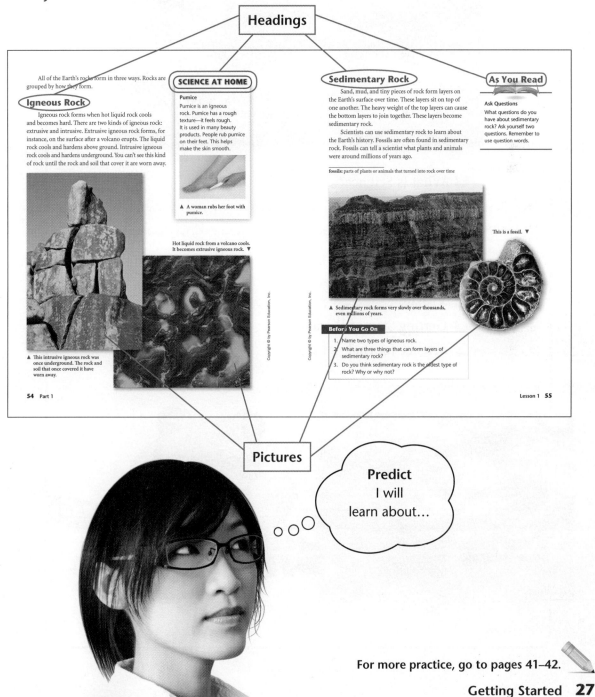

**Headings**

All of the Earth's rocks form in three ways. Rocks are grouped by how they form.

### Igneous Rock

Igneous rock forms when hot liquid rock cools and becomes hard. There are two kinds of igneous rock: extrusive and intrusive. Extrusive igneous rock forms, for instance, on the surface after a volcano erupts. The liquid rock cools and hardens above ground. Intrusive igneous rock cools and hardens underground. You can't see this kind of rock until the rock and soil that cover it are worn away.

▲ This intrusive igneous rock was once underground. The rock and soil that once covered it have worn away.

**SCIENCE AT HOME**

**Pumice**
Pumice is an igneous rock. Pumice has a rough texture—it feels rough. It is used in many beauty products. People rub pumice on their feet. This helps make the skin smooth.

▲ A woman rubs her foot with pumice.

Hot liquid rock from a volcano cools. It becomes extrusive igneous rock. ▼

### Sedimentary Rock

Sand, mud, and tiny pieces of rock form layers on the Earth's surface over time. These layers sit on top of one another. The heavy weight of the top layers can cause the bottom layers to join together. These layers become sedimentary rock.

Scientists can use sedimentary rock to learn about the Earth's history. Fossils are often found in sedimentary rock. Fossils can tell a scientist what plants and animals were around millions of years ago.

**fossils:** parts of plants or animals that turned into rock over time

This is a fossil. ▼

▲ Sedimentary rock forms very slowly over thousands, even millions of years.

**Before You Go On**

1. Name two types of igneous rock.
2. What are three things that can form layers of sedimentary rock?
3. Do you think sedimentary rock is the oldest type of rock? Why or why not?

**As You Read**

**Ask Questions**
What questions do you have about sedimentary rock? Ask yourself two questions. Remember to use question words.

54 Part 1

Lesson 1 **55**

**Pictures**

**Predict**
I will learn about...

For more practice, go to pages 41–42.

# Practice Pages

PRACTICE

# What Is Science?

**A.** Match the parts of the sentence. Write the letter.

_____c____ **1.** Science      **a.** is the Earth and all things on it.

_____ **2.** Scientists      **b.** are things that are alive.

_____ **3.** Living things      **c.** is the study of the natural world.

_____ **4.** Nonliving things      **d.** are people who study our world.

_____ **5.** The world      **e.** are things that are not alive.

**B.** Complete each sentence. Use words from the box.

**1.** _____ is the Earth and all things on it.

**2.** _____ are people who study our world.

**3.** _____ is the study of the natural world.

**4.** _____ are things that are not alive.

**5.** _____ are things that are alive.

> Living things
> Nonliving things
> Science
> Scientists
> The world

**C.** Write *living thing* or *nonliving thing* under each picture.

# The Sciences

**A.** Match the parts of the sentence. Write the letter.

_____d_____ Life science      **a.** is the study of mostly nonliving matter.

_____ **1.** Earth science      **b.** is what living and nonliving things are made of.

_____ **2.** The environment      **c.** is power such as sound, light, and electricity.

_____ **3.** Matter      **d.** is the study of living things.

_____ **4.** Physical science      **e.** is the land, water, air, and living things on the Earth.

_____ **5.** Energy      **f.** is the study of the Earth.

**B.** Write five sentences with words and phrases from the exercise above.

Example: _Life science is the study of living things._____

**1.** _____

**2.** _____

**3.** _____

**4.** _____

**5.** _____

**C.** Circle the word or phrase that doesn't belong.

| | | | |
|---|---|---|---|
| **1.** electricity | energy | (plants) | physical science |
| **2.** life science | rocks | animals | plants |
| **3.** animals | air | rocks | land |
| **4.** Earth science | water | planets | air |
| **5.** energy | sound | light | rocks |
| **6.** humans | electricity | frogs | trees |

Name _____ Date _____

**D.** Under each picture, write the correct kind of science. Choose words from the box.

| Earth science | physical science | life science |
| --- | --- | --- |

_____   _____   _____

_____   _____   _____

**E.** Complete the chart below. Write an example of each kind of science.

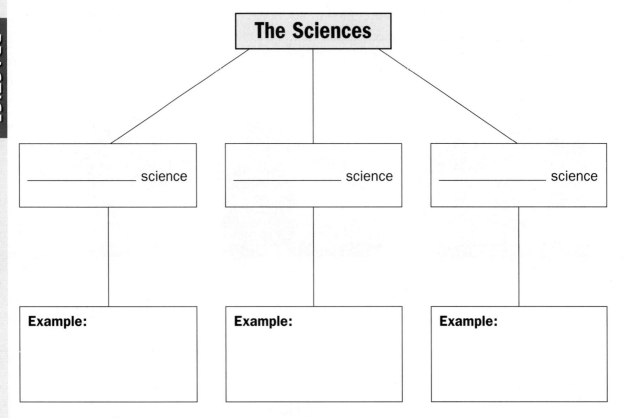

**F.** Choose the best answer. Circle the letter.

**1.** _____ is the study of living things on the Earth.

    **a.** Earth science    **b.** Physical science    **c.** Life science

**2.** The study of energy is part of _____.

    **a.** Earth science    **b.** physical science    **c.** life science

**3.** Our _____ is the land, water, air, and living things around us.

    **a.** living thing    **b.** environment    **c.** sun

**4.** _____ is the study of the Earth.

    **a.** Earth science    **b.** Physical science    **c.** Life science

**5.** _____ is the study of mostly nonliving matter.

    **a.** Earth science    **b.** Physical science    **c.** Life science

Name _____ Date _____

# The Scientific Method

**A.** Write the steps of the scientific method in the correct order. Use the sentences from the box.

> • Draw conclusions.    • Make a hypothesis.
> • Ask questions.       • Observe.
> • Test the hypothesis.

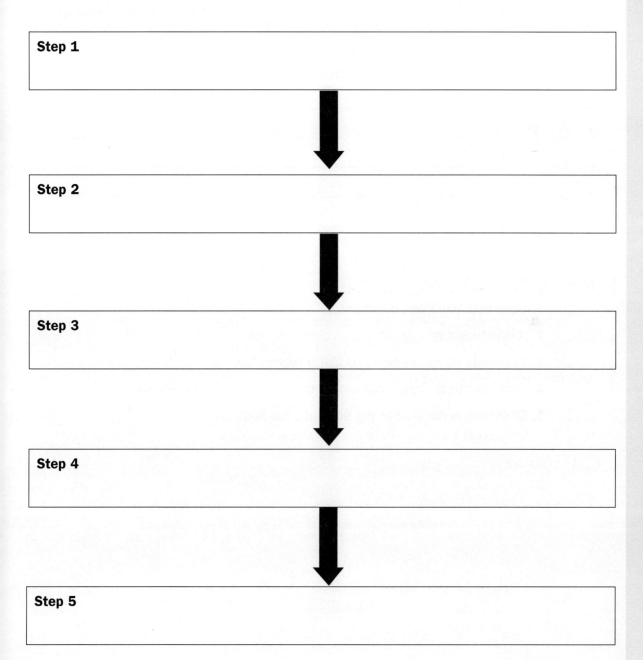

**Step 1**

**Step 2**

**Step 3**

**Step 4**

**Step 5**

**B.** Match the parts of the sentence. Write the letter.

_____ **1.** First, scientists ask questions

_____ **2.** After asking a question,

_____ **3.** After scientists make a hypothesis,

_____ **4.** Scientists observe

_____ **5.** Finally, when scientists draw conclusions,

**a.** scientists make a hypothesis.

**b.** very carefully to see what happens.

**c.** they decide if their hypothesis is correct.

**d.** about things they don't know.

**e.** they test their hypothesis.

**C.** Write five sentences with phrases from the exercise above.

**1.** _____

**2.** _____

**3.** _____

**4.** _____

**5.** _____

**D.** Write T for *true* or F for *false*.

_____ **1.** Scientists don't ask questions.

_____ **2.** A hypothesis is a guess.

_____ **3.** Scientists do experiments to test a hypothesis.

_____ **4.** First scientists draw conclusions, then they make a hypothesis.

_____ **5.** Observing is not part of the scientific method.

# Safety

**A.** Match each safety rule with a picture. Write the letter.

**Safety Rules**

a. Clean up spills.
b. Be careful with scissors.
c. Make sure you understand.
d. Be careful with electricity.

e. Be careful with hot things.
f. Keep things clean.
g. Stay away from broken glass.
h. Tell your teacher if you hurt yourself.

_____

_____

_____

_____

_____

_____

_____

_____

**B.** Match the parts of the sentence. Write the letter.

_____ **1.** Keep          **a.** if anything spills on the floor.

_____ **2.** Stay away      **b.** with scissors.

_____ **3.** Tell your teacher    **c.** electrical cords are out of the way.

_____ **4.** Make sure      **d.** things clean.

_____ **5.** Be careful      **e.** from broken glass.

**C.** Write T for _true_ or F for _false_.

_____ **1.** Always point scissors away from your body.

_____ **2.** Pick up broken glass yourself.

_____ **3.** Don't put things away after an experiment.

_____ **4.** Don't use electrical items near water.

_____ **5.** Don't clean up spills.

**D.** Complete the paragraph. Use words from the box.

| | | | | |
|---|---|---|---|---|
| clean | teacher | understand | hot | electricity |

Safety is very important in the science classroom. You should learn these basic safety rules. Make sure you **(1)** _____ the experiment before you begin. Be careful with **(2)** _____ things. Be careful with **(3)** _____, too. Make sure the cords are out of the way. Keep the experiment area **(4)** _____. Tell your **(5)** _____ if you hurt yourself.

# Science Tools

**VOCABULARY**

**A.** Write the correct word under each picture. Use words from the box.

| camera | hand lens | stopwatch |
| thermometer | microscope | balance |

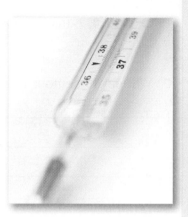

1. _____

2. _____

3. _____

4. _____

5. _____

6. _____

**B.** Match the parts of the sentence. Write the letter.

_____ **1.** A ruler          **a.** lets you see small things close up.

_____ **2.** A hand lens       **b.** lets you see very small things.

_____ **3.** A balance         **c.** lets you measure how hot or cold something is.

_____ **4.** A telescope       **d.** lets you take pictures.

_____ **5.** A stopwatch      **e.** lets you measure how long something is.

_____ **6.** A thermometer    **f.** lets you see things far away.

_____ **7.** A camera        **g.** lets you measure how heavy something is.

_____ **8.** A microscope    **h.** lets you measure time.


**C.** Write eight sentences with words and phrases from the exercise above.

**1.** _____

**2.** _____

**3.** _____

**4.** _____

**5.** _____

**6.** _____

**7.** _____

**8.** _____


**D.** Complete each sentence. Use words from the box.

| thermometer    microscope    telescope    hand lens    ruler |
| --- |

**1.** A _____ has centimeters and inches.

**2.** You hold a _____ in your hand to observe small things.

**3.** A _____ measures how hot or cold something is.

**4.** You look through a _____ to see things that are far away.

**5.** You can observe very, very small things with a _____.

Name _____ Date _____

# Visuals

Write the name of the visual under each picture. Use words or phrases from the box.

| | | | |
|---|---|---|---|
| photograph | cycle diagram | diagram | pie chart |
| illustration | micrograph | chart | sectional diagram |

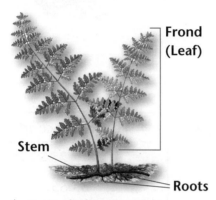

Frond (Leaf)

Stem

Roots

▲ Parts of a fern

1. _____

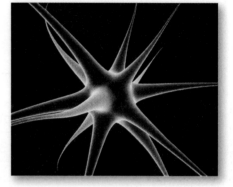

2. _____

3. _____

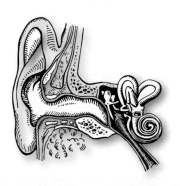

4. _____

5. _____

| Matter | Speed of Sound | |
|---|---|---|
| | Meters per second | Feet per second |
| Dry, cold air | 343 | 1,125 |
| Water | 1,550 | 5,085 |
| Hard wood | 3,960 | 12,992 |
| Glass | 4,540 | 14,895 |
| Steel | 5,050 | 16,568 |

6. _____

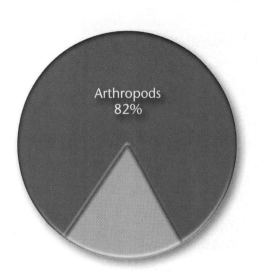

Arthropods
82%

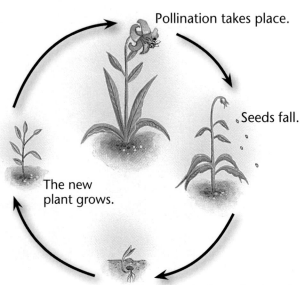

Pollination takes place.

Seeds fall.

The new
plant grows.

Roots and other plant parts
grow out of the seed.

7. _____

8. _____

# Review

## VOCABULARY

Complete the puzzle. Use words from the box.

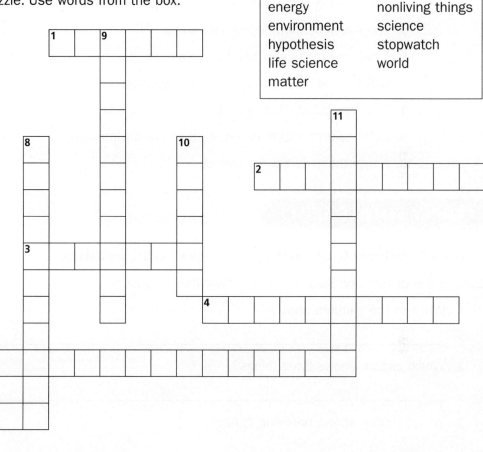

balance
energy
environment
hypothesis
life science
matter

microscope
nonliving things
science
stopwatch
world

**ACROSS**

1. power such as electricity

2. measures time

3. the study of the natural world

4. lets you see very small things

5. things that are not alive

6. measures how heavy something is

**DOWN**

7. Earth and all things on it

8. the study of living things

9. land, water, air, and living things on the Earth

10. what living and nonliving things are made of

11. a scientist's guess

## CHECK YOUR UNDERSTANDING

Write T for *true* or F for *false*.

_______ **1.** Scientists use visuals to share information.

_______ **2.** Physical science is the study of living matter.

_______ **3.** Never tell your teacher if you hurt yourself.

_______ **4.** Life science is the study of living things on the Earth.

_______ **5.** The scientific method has five steps.

_______ **6.** A balance measures how hot something is.

_______ **7.** Safety is not important in the science classroom.

_______ **8.** You draw conclusions at the end of an experiment.

_______ **9.** Earth science includes the study of our environment.

_______ **10.** A hypothesis is always correct.

## APPLY SCIENCE SKILLS

### Science Reading Strategy: Preview and Predict

Look at the pictures on page 2. Then answer the questions.

**1.** What do the pictures show?

_______________________________________________

**2.** Which picture shows living things?

_______________________________________________

**3.** Which picture shows nonliving things?

_______________________________________________

**4.** Predict what you will learn about in your science book.

_______________________________________________

_______________________________________________

_______________________________________________

# Science Journal

Write about five interesting things you have learned in Getting Started.

1. _____
   _____
   _____

2. _____
   _____
   _____

3. _____
   _____
   _____

4. _____
   _____
   _____

5. _____
   _____
   _____

# Rocks and Minerals

## Part Concepts

### Lesson 1
- Rocks cover the Earth.
- Rocks are made of minerals.
- Each mineral has its own properties, or traits.
- Earth is made of four layers of rock and metal.
- There are three kinds of rock: igneous, sedimentary, and metamorphic.

### Lesson 2
- Rocks are always changing.
- Big rocks break down into smaller rocks. This is called weathering.
- Pieces of rock are moved away. This is called erosion.
- Earthquakes and volcanoes move and change rocks.
- Volcanic activity can change other kinds of rock into igneous rock.

## Get Ready

Take a walk outside. Find three rocks with different colors, shapes, and textures. The texture of something is how it feels. Copy the chart below into your notebook. Write information about your rocks in the chart.

| Rock | Color | Shape | Texture |
|------|-------|-------|---------|
| 1 | | | |
| 2 | | | |
| 3 | | | |

## Vocabulary

▲ This is **sedimentary** rock. It is made when sand, mud, and tiny pieces, or **particles**, of rock join together and harden over time. It has layers.

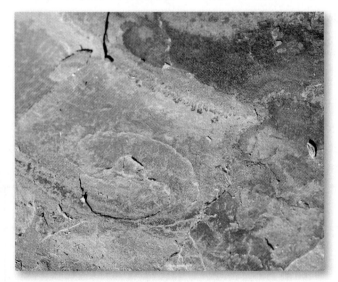

▲ This is **metamorphic** rock. It is made when rock is changed by heat and pressure. Pressure is a force that presses, or pushes.

This is **igneous** rock. It is made from hot liquid rock. ▼

The diamond in this rock is a **mineral**. A diamond is clear and very hard. These are two of its **properties**, or traits. ▼

Key Words

igneous

metamorphic

mineral

properties

sedimentary

volcano

▲ This **volcano** is erupting. Hot liquid rock is coming out of the ground.

## Practice

Choose the word that completes each sentence.

1. A diamond is clear and very hard. These are two of its _____.
   **a.** properties      **b.** volcano      **c.** mineral

2. When a _____ erupts, hot liquid rock comes out of the ground.
   **a.** mineral      **b.** volcano      **c.** metamorphic

3. A diamond is one type of _____.
   **a.** volcano      **b.** properties      **c.** mineral

4. _____ rock is sand, mud, and tiny pieces of rock joined together.
   **a.** Igneous      **b.** Metamorphic      **c.** Sedimentary

5. Hot liquid rock makes _____ rock.
   **a.** sedimentary      **b.** igneous      **c.** metamorphic

6. _____ rock is made when rock is changed by heat and pressure.
   **a.** Metamorphic      **b.** Sedimentary      **c.** Igneous

---

**particles:** very small pieces

For more practice, go to page 61.

# Science Skills

## Science Reading Strategy: **Ask Questions**

When you read, **ask questions.**

- Asking questions helps you understand what you read.
- Ask questions with the words *What, Why, Where, When,* and *How.*

Read the text below. After each sentence, ask and answer a question from the chart.

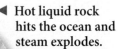

◀ Hot liquid rock hits the ocean and steam explodes.

There are black sand beaches on the Big Island of Hawaii. The sand is black because it is made of dark igneous rock. Many years ago, a volcano erupted. Hot liquid rock poured out of the volcano. The sand was created as this rock broke down into smaller and smaller pieces.

Black sand beach in Hawaii ▼

| Question Words | Questions |
|---|---|
| **Where** | **Where** are the black sand beaches? |
| **Why** | **Why** is the sand black? |
| **When** | **When** did a volcano erupt? |
| **What** | **What** poured out of the volcano? |
| **How** | **How** was the sand made? |

Look for an **As You Read** activity in the lesson. It will help you understand the lesson.

For more practice, go to pages 62–63.

## Using Visuals: **Sectional Diagrams**

A sectional diagram shows what the inside of something looks like.
This diagram shows how the Earth looks deep inside. The Earth has four
layers. Two of these layers are solid, or hard. The other two layers are not.
The colors show how hot each layer is.

Look at the diagram and the color key. Then answer the questions.

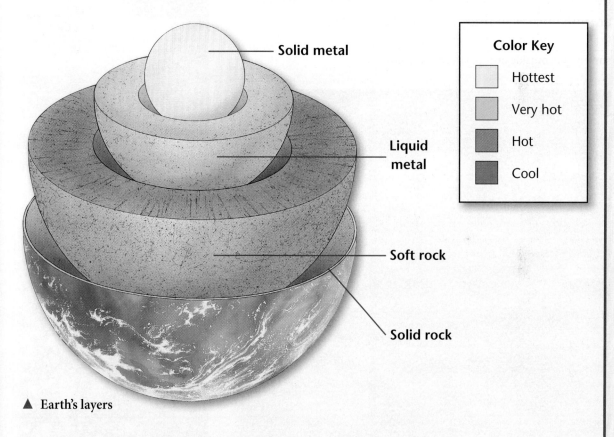

Solid metal

Liquid
metal

Soft rock

Solid rock

**Color Key**

Hottest

Very hot

Hot

Cool

▲ Earth's layers

1. What is the hottest layer made of?

2. What is the coolest layer made of?

3. Which layers are not solid?

For more practice, go to page 64.

## Lesson ❶

# What Are Rocks and Minerals?

Rocks cover the Earth's **surface**. Many of them are under water, ice, or soil. Everywhere you go, there are rocks. Mountains are made of very large rocks. Many beaches are made up of tiny rocks called sand. Streams are good places to find rocks of all different sizes.

---

**surface:** the outside or top part of something

▲ This stream has rocks of different sizes.

▲ Some rocks are very big.

▲ Sand is made of many tiny rocks.

All rocks are made of minerals. Most rocks are made up of several minerals. But some rocks are made up of only one or two minerals.

A mineral has certain properties that tell you it's a mineral. It must be solid, or hard. This solid mineral must have **crystals**. A mineral must also come from nature, or happen naturally. You probably know the mineral halite—it's salt.

---

crystals: shapes that repeat and are all the same in a mineral, rock, or other solid

**LANGUAGE TIP**

nature    →   noun

natural   →   adjective

naturally →   adverb

**LEARN MORE ABOUT IT**

The atoms that make up a mineral line up in a regular pattern. This pattern repeats over and over. The repeating pattern of a mineral's atoms forms a mineral's crystal structure. All the crystals of a mineral have the same crystal structure. Scientists can use crystal structure to identify very small mineral samples.

This rock is made of rock salt and sand. ▼

▲ Halite (salt) crystals are shaped like boxes.

**Before You Go On**

1. Name three places you can find rocks.
2. Name three properties all minerals have.
3. Can something made by a person be a mineral? Why or why not?

There are about 3,800 minerals. Each mineral has different properties. So each mineral has different uses. For example, the mineral copper can carry **electricity**. Copper can be shaped easily. Because of these properties, copper makes good wire.

Diamonds are the hardest mineral. You can see through diamonds. When diamonds are cut, they shine. Because of these properties, diamonds make beautiful gems.

---

**electricity:** a form of energy that can travel through wire

▼ This copper has been made into wire.

▲ Pieces of copper

◄ Diamonds make beautiful gems.

**HEALTH CONNECTION**

**Minerals We Eat**

There are small amounts of minerals in many of the foods we eat. Some of these minerals help our bodies grow and stay healthy. Calcium, for example, helps us build strong bones. Milk, cheese, and many green vegetables all have a lot of calcium.

▲ These foods are rich in the mineral calcium.

About twenty kinds of minerals make up most of the Earth's rocks. These minerals can be found in any of the Earth's four layers.

The first layer is the crust, or the Earth's surface. It is made of rock. This rock is under the water, sand, and soil and is exposed at the surface. The next layer is called the mantle. It is made of hot soft rock.

The third layer is the outer core. It is made mostly of liquid metal. The center of the Earth is the inner core. It is made of solid metal. The inner core is the hottest part of the Earth.

## SCIENCE NOW

**Using the Earth's Heat**

Rock below the Earth's surface is very hot. The hot rock heats up areas of underground water. The water can get as hot as 700° Fahrenheit. Power companies use drills to reach this water. They use the water's heat to make electricity. This photo shows part of the drills.

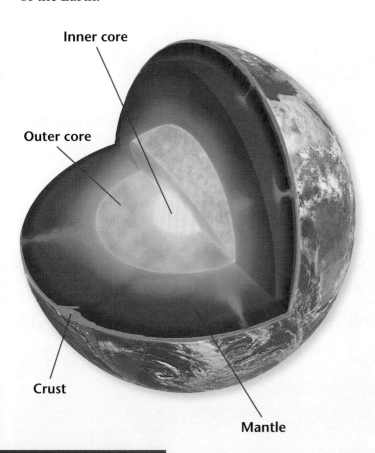

Inner core

Outer core

Crust

Mantle

### Before You Go On

1. What are two properties of copper?
2. Name the four layers of the Earth.
3. When a volcano erupts, hot liquid rock comes out. From which layer does this liquid rock originate, or begin?

All of the Earth's rocks form in three ways. Rocks are grouped by how they form.

# Igneous Rock

Igneous rock forms when hot liquid rock cools and becomes hard. There are two kinds of igneous rock: extrusive and intrusive. Extrusive igneous rock forms, for instance, on the surface after a volcano erupts. The liquid rock cools and hardens above ground. Intrusive igneous rock cools and hardens underground. You can't see this kind of rock until the rock and soil that cover it are worn away.

Hot liquid rock from a volcano cools. It becomes extrusive igneous rock. ▼

▲ This intrusive igneous rock was once underground. The rock and soil that once covered it have worn away.

**54**   Part 1

# Sedimentary Rock

Sand, mud, and tiny pieces of rock form layers on the Earth's surface over time. These layers sit on top of one another. The heavy weight of the top layers can cause the bottom layers to join together. These layers become sedimentary rock.

Scientists can use sedimentary rock to learn about the Earth's history. **Fossils** are often found in sedimentary rock. Fossils can tell a scientist what plants and animals were around millions of years ago.

---

**fossils:** parts of plants or animals that turned into rock over time

## As You Read

**Ask Questions**

What questions do you have about sedimentary rock? Ask yourself two questions. Remember to use question words.

This is a fossil. ▼

▲ Sedimentary rock forms very slowly over thousands, even millions of years.

## Before You Go On

1. Name two types of igneous rock.
2. What are three things that can form layers of sedimentary rock?
3. Do you think sedimentary rock is the oldest type of rock? Why or why not?

# Metamorphic Rock

Deep underground, there is a lot of heat and pressure. This heat and pressure can change igneous and sedimentary rock into another type of rock called metamorphic rock. Metamorphic rock often has layers that fold over one another. Marble and slate are metamorphic rocks. These rocks are used in many buildings.

**LANGUAGE TIP**

**metamorphic** = "change" + "form"

The prefix *meta-* means "change." The root *-morph-* means "form."

▲ This metamorphic rock is called gneiss (neyes).

▲ The Taj Mahal is in India. It is made of marble.

# Exploring

## The Rock Cycle

Rocks are always changing. The changes happen slowly. Over thousands of years, rock breaks down into sand. Then the sand can become sedimentary rock. And sedimentary rock can change into metamorphic or igneous rock. All rock that is deep underground can be melted, or turned into liquid rock. The liquid rock is then returned to the Earth's surface when a volcano erupts. As the liquid rock cools, new igneous rock forms. This process is called the rock cycle.

Igneous rock

Breaks down into sand

Sedimentary rock

Melting

Heat and pressure

Melting

Breaks down into sand

Heat and pressure

Volcanic activity

Liquid rock

Metamorphic rock

Melting

## Before You Go On

1. Where does metamorphic rock form?
2. What are two examples of metamorphic rock?
3. Why is rock good for making buildings?

# Lesson ❶ – Review and Practice

## Vocabulary

Complete each sentence with the correct word from the box.

| properties | metamorphic | volcano | igneous | sedimentary | mineral |

1. Hot liquid rock cools and forms _____ rock.

2. Mud, sand, and pieces of rock join together in layers to form _____ rock.

3. Marble and slate are _____ rocks.

4. A _____ helps to form igneous rock.

5. Copper is a _____.

6. Each mineral has its own _____.

## Check Your Understanding

Write the answer to each question.

1. What are all rocks made of? _____

2. What are the four layers of the Earth? _____

3. How does metamorphic rock form? _____

4. What does the rock cycle show? _____

## Apply Science Skills

### Science Reading Strategy: Ask Questions

Reread pages 50–53. As you read, ask yourself questions. Write your questions in the chart.

| What |
|------|
| Why |
| Where |

## Using Visuals: **Sectional Diagrams**

This sectional diagram shows the inside of a volcano. It also shows how the two types of igneous rock are formed.

Look at the diagram. Then answer the questions.

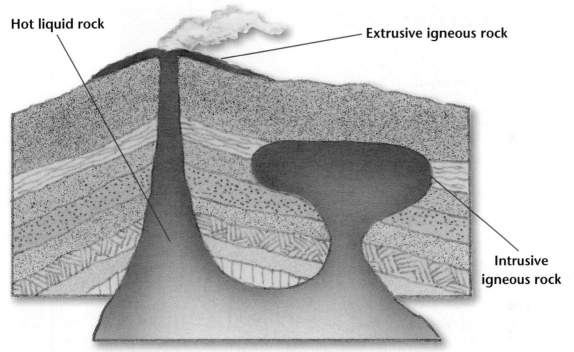

Hot liquid rock

Extrusive igneous rock

Intrusive igneous rock

▲ Two types of igneous rock

1. Which type of rock cools and hardens above the ground? _____

2. Which type of rock cools and hardens below the ground? _____

3. Where does the hot liquid rock come from? _____

_____

## Discuss

What are some things in your home or school that are made of rock? What kind of rock do you think it is? What other things do people make or build out of rock?

For more practice, go to pages 65–66.

# Practice Pages

# Before You Read

## VOCABULARY

**A.** Match each key word with its definition. Write the letter.

_____ **1.** properties      **a.** rock formed from hot liquid rock

_____ **2.** igneous      **b.** rock made from sand, mud, and pieces of rock

_____ **3.** metamorphic      **c.** traits

_____ **4.** mineral      **d.** rock made from rock that is changed by heat and pressure

_____ **5.** sedimentary      **e.** nonliving substance that rock is made of

**B.** Write five sentences using each key word and its definition.

**1.** _____

**2.** _____

**3.** _____

**4.** _____

**5.** _____

**C.** Circle the correct word or phrase to complete each sentence.

**1.** A rock changed by heat and pressure is called a (trait / metamorphic) rock.

**2.** When a (diamond / volcano) erupts, hot liquid rock comes out of the ground.

**3.** (Igneous / Sedimentary) rock is made of sand, mud, and very small pieces of rock.

**4.** A diamond is a (metamorphic rock / mineral).

**5.** Rock made from hot liquid rock is (igneous / sedimentary) rock.

**D.** Write T for *true* or F for *false*. Correct the sentences that are false.

_____ **1.** A diamond is clear and soft.

_____ **2.** Metamorphic rock is rock changed by heat and pressure.

_____ **3.** Sedimentary rock is made from hot liquid rock.

_____ **4.** Igneous rock can form a volcano.

_____ **5.** Hot liquid rock erupts out of a diamond.

## Science Reading Strategy: Ask Questions

**A.** You just learned to ask questions as you read. Read the paragraph below. Write questions using *What, Where, Why,* and *How.* Then write your answers.

The Earth has four layers. On the outermost layer is where we live. This layer is called the crust. The crust is like the shell of an egg. It is thin compared to the other layers. It is only 3–47 miles thick. The crust is made of lighter materials than the other layers. Heavier materials sink down, so they end up deep inside the Earth.

| Question Words | Questions and Answers |
|---|---|
| What | |
| Where | |
| Why | |
| How | |

**B.** Now share your questions and answers with a partner.

## Science Reading Strategy: Ask Questions

**A.** Read the paragraph below. Write questions using *What, When, Where,* and *How.*
Then write your answers.

Minerals have several common properties. They are found in the Earth.
They are nonliving. They are made up of specific groups of atoms. They are solid,
and they can grow crystals. Minerals such as gold, silver, and copper are found in
the rocks of ancient volcanoes. A very long time ago, humans discovered some of
these minerals and used them to make jewelry and tools.

| Question Words | Questions and Answers |
|---|---|
| What | |
| When | |
| Where | |
| How | |

**B.** Now share your questions and answers with a partner.

# Using Visuals: Sectional Diagrams

Look at the sectional diagram of the Earth's layers. Then answer the questions.

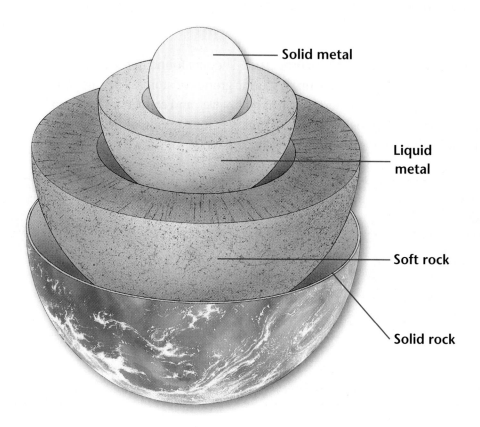

1. How many layers do you see in this sectional diagram?

_____

2. What are the two inner layers made of?

_____

3. What are the two outer layers made of?

_____

4. Which layer is made of rock that is not solid?

_____

5. Which layer is at the center of the Earth?

_____

# Lesson 1 Review

## VOCABULARY

PRACTICE

Complete the puzzle. Use key words. Write the secret word.

1. A mineral's traits are called _____.

   ◯— __ __ __ __ __ __ __ __

2. Volcanoes make _____ rock.

   __ __ __ __ __◯__

3. Heat and pressure change rock into _____ rock.

   __ __ __ __◯__ __ __ __ __

4. Some _____ rock is made of sand.

   __ __ __◯__ __ __ __ __ __

5. A _____ erupts.

   __ __ __◯__ __ __

6. A diamond is made of one _____.

   __ __ __◯__ __ __

**Secret word:** ___ ___ ___ ___ ___ ___ (a kind of igneous rock)

## VOCABULARY IN CONTEXT

Complete the paragraph. Use words from the box. There is one extra word.

| igneous | volcano | sedimentary | metamorphic |
|---|---|---|---|

A **(1)** _____ is a mountain that erupts. Hot liquid rock comes out.

When it cools, it forms **(2)** _____ rock. This rock can change. Heat and

pressure can change it into **(3)** _____ rock.

## CHECK YOUR UNDERSTANDING

Choose the best answer. Circle the letter.

1. Sedimentary rock is tiny pieces of rock, _____ joined together.

   **a.** mud, and sand      **b.** water, and halite      **c.** copper, and iron

2. The surface of the Earth is called the _____.

   **a.** inner core          **b.** crust                  **c.** mantle

3. About twenty kinds of _____ make up most of the Earth's rocks.

   **a.** diamonds           **b.** liquids                **c.** minerals

4. The inner core is made of _____ metal.

   **a.** soft               **b.** liquid                 **c.** solid

## Science Reading Strategy: Ask Questions

Read the paragraph below. Write questions using *What, Why, Where,* and *How.* Then write your answers.

> The Earth has four layers. The first layer is the crust. This is the ground where you stand. Next to the crust is the mantle. It is made of hot, soft rock. Forces inside the Earth push this soft rock up through a volcano's opening. The next layer is the outer core. It is made of liquid metal that flows continuously around the inner core. The inner core is made of solid metal. Scientists cannot go inside the last three layers to study them because they are too deep and too hot.

| Question Words | Questions and Answers |
|---|---|
| What | |
| Why | |
| Where | |
| How | |

## Using Visuals: Sectional Diagrams

Look at the diagram on page 59. Then answer the questions.

1. What does the diagram show?

   _____

2. What is coming out of the volcano?

   _____

3. What are two types of igneous rock in the diagram?

   _____

4. Can igneous rock be formed in any other way?

   _____

5. Do you think this volcano is active? Why or why not?

   _____

PRACTICE

# Science Journal

Write about five interesting things you have learned in this lesson.

1. _____

_____

_____

2. _____

_____

_____

3. _____

_____

_____

4. _____

_____

_____

5. _____

_____

_____

## Vocabulary

The study of rocks is called **geology**. A scientist who studies rocks is a **geologist**. ▼

▲ In an **earthquake**, the ground moves, or shakes. This is a building after a strong earthquake.

◀ Wind and water caused pieces of this rock to break off. This is called **weathering**. Then wind and water moved the pieces away. This is called **erosion**.

The big sheet of ice on this mountain is a **glacier**.
When glaciers move, they move pieces of rock. ▼

*Key Words*

**earthquake**

**erosion**

**geologist**

**geology**

**glacier**

**weathering**

## Practice

Next to each key word, write its meaning. Use your own words.

1. earthquake _a violent shaking of the Earth's crust_

2. erosion _____

3. glacier _____

4. geologist _____

5. geology _____

6. weathering _____

For more practice, go to page 83.

Lesson 2  **69**

# Science Skills

## Science Reading Strategy: **Cause and Effect**

When you read, it is important to understand **cause and effect**.

- A cause makes something happen. The effect is what happens.
- Look for the words *caused*, *because of*, or *as a result.* These words often tell about cause and effect.

   Read this text. As you read, look for cause and effect.

Earthquakes make the ground move. Sometimes they are very dangerous. In 1995, there was a very strong earthquake in the city of Kobe, Japan. The earthquake caused many buildings to fall. The earthquake also caused many fires. Over 5,000 people died because of this earthquake.

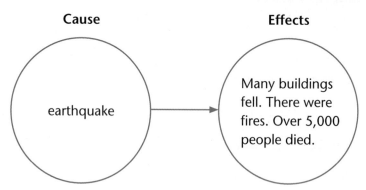

| Cause | | Effects |
|-------|--|---------|
| earthquake | → | Many buildings fell. There were fires. Over 5,000 people died. |

Look for an **As You Read** question in the lesson. It will ask you to find cause and effect. It will help you understand the lesson.

For more practice, go to pages 84–85.

## Using Visuals: **Photo Sequences**

A photo sequence shows an event in two or more photographs. This photo sequence shows a tsunami (soo-NAH-mee). A tsunami is a very big wave often caused by an earthquake under the ocean. A tsunami hit southeastern Asia on December 26, 2004. These photos show the land before and after the tsunami.

Look at the photos and captions. Then answer the questions.

▲ Banda Aceh, Indonesia, April 12, 2004

▲ Banda Aceh, Indonesia, January 2, 2005

1. What does the land look like before the tsunami?

2. What does the land look like after the tsunami?

3. How did the tsunami change the land?

**For more practice, go to page 86.**

# Lesson 2

# The Earth's Changing Surface

## Weathering

Rocks are always changing. One way in which rocks change is called weathering. Weathering is the breaking down of rocks into pieces. Weathering is a very slow process. It can take thousands of years.

Many things cause weathering. Water can get inside the cracks of a rock. When the water freezes, pieces of rock can break off. Wind and rain beat on rocks and make them weak. The salt in the sea and the oxygen in the air also weaken rock. Then the rock breaks down.

▲ Rocks break down. This process is called weathering.

Animals and plants can also cause weathering. Animal waste can help break down rock. Plants can grow inside cracks. This pressure can cause the rock to break apart.

▲ Bird droppings are making this rock weak.

▲ This rock is being weathered by a tree root.

### Before You Go On

1. How does weathering change rock?
2. How can water cause weathering?
3. Do you think weathering is part of the rock cycle? Why or why not?

# Erosion

First rock is weathered. Then wind, water, or ice carries the loose pieces of rock away. This process is called erosion. Wind can carry sand and small pieces of rock very far. Rivers can move rocks and soil from a mountaintop to the sea. Glaciers also carry rocks and soil. A glacier moves slowly down a mountain. It melts and refreezes many times. As a glacier moves, it picks up rocks and soil and carries them along.

▼ Glaciers can move rocks and soil.

## SCIENCE AT HOME

**Rounded Rocks**

Many rocks have rounded edges. How did they get their shape? They were weathered and eroded. River or ocean water flowed over these rocks for a long time. As the water flowed, the rocks hit against one another. The rough edges were smoothed down. Find a rounded rock and bring it to class.

◄ Wind can blow sand a long way.

As a result of weathering and erosion, the land begins to look different. Wind can cause sand to build up in new places. Sand blown by the wind can wear away a rock. This changes the rock's shape. Waves crash against big rocks again and again. In time, the waves can make a hole in the rock.

▲ Water changed the shape of this rock.

◄ Windblown sand changed the shape of this rock.

**Soil Erosion**

Rain washes soil down hills. Plants like grass and trees help to keep soil in place. But in some places, the grass and trees have been destroyed. Without plants, rain may carry rich soil away from farming sites. This can harm a country's food supply.

▲ Eroded hillside in Guatemala

**LEARN MORE ABOUT IT**

Rock in Earth's crust is always changing. Forces deep inside Earth and at the surface produce a slow cycle that builds, destroys, and changes the rock in the crust. The rock cycle is a series of processes that occur on Earth's surface and in the crust and mantle that slowly change rocks from one kind to another. For example, weathering can break down granite into sediment that later forms sandstone.

**Before You Go On**

1. What are two examples of erosion?
2. How is erosion different from weathering?
3. How can weathering and erosion change the shape of rock?

# Earthquakes

Pressure builds up under the Earth's crust. This can cause pieces of the Earth's crust to move. When this happens, the ground shakes. This is an earthquake. Rocks can break and move during an earthquake.

The Earth's crust has large faults, or cracks, in it. Earthquakes often happen along these faults. Most earthquakes don't last long. But some earthquakes are very strong. They can cause great damage.

**Cause and Effect**

What causes an earthquake? Name one effect of an earthquake.

▲ Earthquakes can damage towns and cities.

▲ This is a fault in California.

Very strong earthquakes under the ocean can cause big waves to form. These waves are called tsunami. If a tsunami reaches land, it can be very dangerous. It can cover everything in water and cause a lot of damage. A tsunami can kill people, animals, and plants.

**LANGUAGE TIP**

The word *tsunami* is Japanese. Its plural and singular forms are the same.

▲ This damage was caused by a tsunami.

## Before You Go On

1. Where do earthquakes often happen?
2. What can cause a tsunami?
3. How can earthquakes and tsunami change the land?

# Volcanoes

A volcano is a deep hole in the surface of the Earth. Pressure builds up inside the volcano. This pressure causes liquid rock from inside the Earth to burst out.

A volcano can erupt violently. Sometimes the rock from its mountain explodes. As a result, liquid rock, **ash**, and hard rock cover the land around the volcano. The liquid rock cools and hardens into new igneous rock. This is why most volcanoes have a mountain of hardened rock and ash around them.

---

**ash:** gray powder that is left after something is burned

Hole of a volcano ▶

## *Leaders in Science*

### Sir Charles Lyell (1797–1875)

Sir Charles Lyell was one of the first geologists to understand that rock and land usually change slowly over time. Before Lyell, people believed that land was shaped mostly by big events such as earthquakes and volcanoes. Lyell taught modern principles, or concepts, of geology. He helped people understand that rock changes gradually, as a result of everyday weather and events.

Some volcanoes are active. This means that they can erupt at any time. It is not safe to live close to an active volcano. It is hard to know exactly when the volcano will erupt. There are a number of active volcanoes in the United States. One of these is Mount St. Helens, in the state of Washington.

◄ Mount St. Helens before 1980 eruption

◄ Mount St. Helens erupting

The land around Mount St. Helens soon after eruption ▶

## HISTORY CONNECTION

**A City Is Destroyed**

Pompeii was an ancient Roman city. A volcano destroyed it in 79 C.E. Ash and liquid rock covered the city. Most of the people of Pompeii died.

▲ A victim in Pompeii covers her face during the eruption.

## Before You Go On

1. What causes a volcano to erupt?
2. Name an active volcano.
3. Why do most volcanoes have a mountain of hardened rock and ash around them?

# Lesson ②—Review and Practice—

## Vocabulary

Complete each sentence with the correct word from the box. Write the sentences in your notebook.

| | | |
|---|---|---|
| erosion | glacier | earthquake |
| geologist | geology | weathering |

1. A _____ is a big sheet of ice.

2. A person who studies rocks is a _____.

3. The ground shakes during an _____.

4. The breaking down of rock into pieces is called _____.

5. Wind and water moving loose pieces of rock is called _____.

6. _____ is the study of rocks.

## Check Your Understanding

Write the answer to each question.

1. What are four things that cause weathering? _____

2. What are three things that cause erosion? _____

3. What causes an earthquake? _____

4. What type of rock is usually around a volcano? Why? _____

## Apply Science Skills

### Science Reading Strategy: **Cause and Effect**

Reread page 77. Complete the diagram.

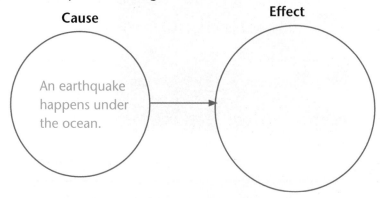

Cause

Effect

An earthquake happens under the ocean.

## Using Visuals: **Photo Sequences**

This photo sequence shows how water changed the shape of rock over time. Look at the photo sequence. Then answer the questions.

The waves wear away the back of the cave. The rock now has a new shape. It is an arch. ▼

▲ Waves hit the rock again and again. This forms a hole. The hole gets bigger and becomes a cave.

◄ Over time, the waves wear away the top of the arch. Finally, all that is left is a tall piece of rock.

1. What causes a cave to form? What causes an arch to form?

_____

2. What happens when waves wear away the top of the arch?

_____

# Discuss

Look again at the photo sequence above. What do you think will happen to the tall piece of rock over time?

**For more practice, go to pages 87–88.**

# Practice Pages

PRACTICE

# Before You Read

## VOCABULARY

**A.** Draw an arrow from each key word to its definition.

| | |
|---|---|
| **1.** weathering | the movement of rocks and soil |
| **2.** geologist | the breaking up of rock into pieces |
| **3.** erosion | a shaking of the ground |
| **4.** earthquake | a big sheet of ice |
| **5.** glacier | a person who studies rocks |

**B.** Write five sentences using each key word and its definition.

**1.** _____

**2.** _____

**3.** _____

**4.** _____

**5.** _____

**C.** Write T for *true* or F for *false.* Correct the sentences that are false.

_____ **1.** An earthquake shakes the ground. _____

_____ **2.** Weathering is the study of weather. _____

_____ **3.** Geology is the study of rocks. _____

_____ **4.** Wind, water, and glaciers can cause geology. _____

_____ **5.** A glacier is a big sheet of sand. _____

**D.** Circle the word or phrase that doesn't belong.

| | | | |
|---|---|---|---|
| **1.** wind | ice | earthquake | water |
| **2.** geology | life science | rocks | geologist |
| **3.** earthquake | building | shake | sand |
| **4.** tsunami | volcano | erosion | earthquake |
| **5.** glacier | water | igneous | ice |

PRACTICE

## Science Reading Strategy: Cause and Effect

**A.** Read the paragraph. As you read, look for cause and effect. Then answer
the questions.

Heavy rain or an earthquake can cause a mudslide. Mudslides can cause
severe damage to cities. In January 2004, in Ventura County, California, a big
mudslide destroyed many houses and trees. The mudslide damaged roads, too.
Several people died as a result of this mudslide.

**1.** What can heavy rain or an earthquake cause?

_____

**2.** What are some effects of a mudslide?

_____

**B.** Complete the diagram below. Write the effects in the circle on the right.

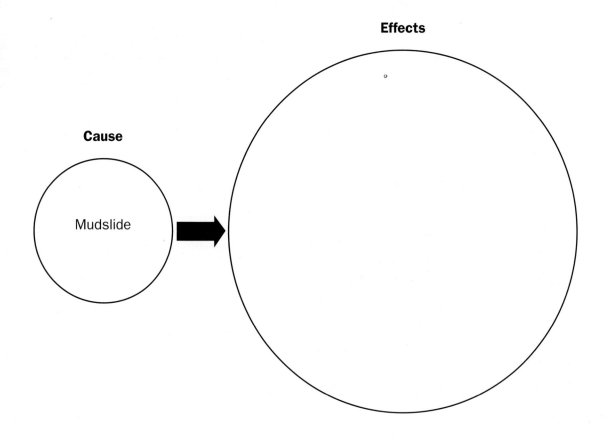

**Effects**

**Cause**

Mudslide

PRACTICE

## Science Reading Strategy: Cause and Effect

**A.** Read the paragraph. As you read, look for cause and effect. Then answer the questions.

> In some developing countries, people cut down a lot of trees. This is called deforestation. Deforestation has several bad effects on the land and the people who live on it. When there are no trees, strong rains can cause mudslides. Deforestation can also cause erosion of the soil. The soil moves because there are no tree roots to hold it down. Animals that live in the trees go to other locations. Soon the land is no longer useful to plants, animals, or humans.

**1.** What is deforestation?

_____

**2.** What causes soil erosion?

_____

**B.** Complete the diagram below. Write one effect in each box.

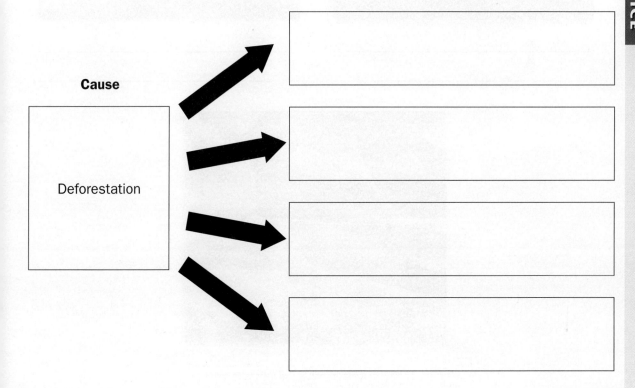

**Effects**

**Cause**

Deforestation

# Using Visuals: Photo Sequences

**A.** You learned that a photo sequence shows an event in two or more photographs. Read the paragraph below.

> First the volcano erupts. Hot liquid rock comes out. Then the hot liquid rock cools and hardens, forming igneous rock. Over time, formations of igneous rock may develop above the ground.

**B.** Now write sentences from the paragraph to label each photo. Then number the photos to make a sequence.

_____

_____

_____

_____

_____

_____

# Lesson 2 Review

## VOCABULARY

Use the words in the box to identify each clue. Write the word on the line.

| erosion    glacier    earthquake    geologist    weathering |

**1.** I am a scientist who studies rocks. _____

**2.** I am a big sheet of ice. _____

**3.** I make the ground shake. _____

**4.** I am the breaking of rock into pieces. _____

**5.** I am the moving of soil and rocks. _____

## VOCABULARY IN CONTEXT

Complete the paragraph. Use words from the box. There is one extra word.

| weathering    earthquakes    geologist    glacier |

The Earth's surface changes over time. **(1)** A _____ studies these changes. He or she studies how wind, water, and animals break down rock. This is called **(2)** _____. Geologists also study the movement of the Earth's crust. Strong movements are called **(3)** _____. They can cause a lot of damage.

## CHECK YOUR UNDERSTANDING

Choose the best answer. Circle the letter.

**1.** An earthquake often happens along a _____.

    **a.** fault    **b.** road    **c.** volcano

**2.** A volcano erupts when _____.

    **a.** weathering occurs    **b.** a glacier melts    **c.** pressure builds

**3.** _____ can change the shape of the land.

    **a.** Erosion    **b.** Geologists    **c.** Animals

**4.** A tsunami can occur as a result of _____.

    **a.** a rock cycle    **b.** a glacier    **c.** an earthquake

## Science Reading Strategy: Cause and Effect

Read the paragraph. Write the effects in the diagram.

A mountaintop is a good place to see the effects of weathering. Mountaintops are exposed to air, wind, and water. Over time, these forces cause the rock surface to break up into pieces. Many mountains are covered by plantlike things called lichens (LEYE-kuhnz). Lichens produce chemicals that also cause rock to break apart.

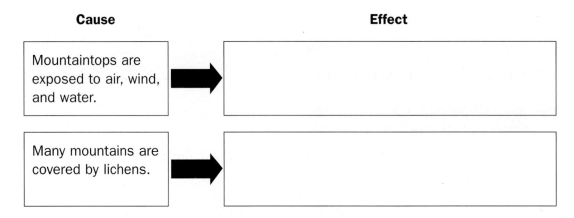

| Cause | Effect |
|---|---|
| Mountaintops are exposed to air, wind, and water. | |
| Many mountains are covered by lichens. | |

## Using Visuals: Photo Sequences

Look at the pictures below. Then answer the questions.

a.

b.

c.

1. These photos are not in the correct sequence. What is the correct sequence?

_____

2. What does this photo sequence show?

_____

# Science Journal

Write about five interesting things you have learned in this lesson.

1. _____

   _____

   _____

2. _____

   _____

   _____

3. _____

   _____

   _____

4. _____

   _____

   _____

5. _____

   _____

   _____

# Part Review

## Vocabulary

Answer the questions with words from the box.

| | | | |
|---|---|---|---|
| geology | weathering | mineral | sedimentary |
| volcano | properties | erosion | glacier |
| earthquake | igneous | metamorphic | geologist |

1. When does hot liquid rock come out of the ground? _____

2. What kind of rock is made from hot liquid rock? _____

3. What kind of rock is made from sand, mud, and tiny pieces of rock? _____

4. What kind of rock is marble? _____

5. What is the study of rocks called? _____

6. What is halite? _____

7. What do all minerals have? _____

8. What is a large sheet of ice called? _____

9. When does the ground shake? _____

10. What is the breaking down of rocks called? _____

11. What happens when wind and water move pieces of rock? _____

12. What is a person who studies rocks called? _____

## Check Your Understanding

Write T for *true* or F for *false* for each statement. Rewrite each false statement to make it correct.

_____ 1. Marble and slate are igneous rocks. _____

_____ 2. The center of the Earth is solid. _____

_____ 3. A volcano can help make new rock. _____

_____ 4. Glaciers cannot move rocks. _____

# Extension Project

Collect small rocks from around your school or home. Compare your rocks to pictures in reference books or on the Internet. Try to figure out what kind of rock each one is.

# Apply Science Skills

## Using Visuals: **Sectional Diagrams**

Look at this sectional diagram of liquid rock being brought to the Earth's surface. Then look at the labels below it. Next to each label, write the correct number.

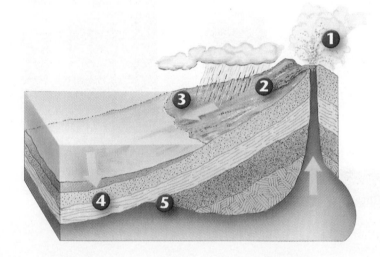

_____ Liquid rock from the volcano cools and hardens.

_____ The heavy weight of the top layers causes the igneous rock to form sedimentary rock.

_____ Wind, water, and plants weather the rock and move it downhill into the ocean.

_____ A volcanic eruption brings liquid rock to the surface of the Earth.

_____ Hot liquid rock inside the Earth melts the sedimentary rock.

# Part Experiment

## How Do Rocks Change?

Remember what you learned about the rock cycle. One kind of rock can turn into another kind of rock.

## Purpose

To make models of the rocks in the rock cycle

## Materials

crayons
pencil sharpener
plastic wrap
cutting board
microwave oven
oven mitt
spatula

## What to Do

1. Choose three different colored crayons.

2. Onto a piece of plastic wrap, shave the first crayon with the pencil sharpener. Now do the same with the second and third crayon. Each color is like a layer of rock.

3. Fold the plastic wrap over the crayon shavings. Now put the wooden board on top of the shavings. Push down.

4. Now put the "rock" and plastic wrap in the microwave oven. Heat it until it melts.

5. Put on the oven mitt. Use the spatula to take the "liquid rock" out of the oven. Be careful not to burn yourself. Let the "liquid rock" cool completely before you touch it.

## Draw Conclusions

1. What kind of "rock" did you make in Step 3? Explain.

2. What kind of "rock" did you make in Steps 4 and 5? Explain.

Work with a partner. Discuss your conclusions. Then write them under Step 5 on page 94.

# Experiment Log:
# How Do Rocks Change?

Follow the steps of the scientific method as you do your experiment.
Write notes about each step as the experiment progresses.

**Step 1: Ask questions.**

**Step 2: Make a hypothesis.**

**Step 3: Test your hypothesis.**

**Step 4: Observe.**

**Step 5: Draw conclusions.**

# Write About It

1. You learned about diamonds in this unit. What are some properties of diamonds? Why do you think people value them so highly?

_____

_____

_____

_____

_____

_____

_____

_____

2. Rocks are strong. But water can wear away rock over time. Write a story about a contest between two characters—Rock and Water. Which character is stronger?

_____

_____

_____

_____

_____

_____

_____

_____

# Planets and Stars

## Part Concepts

### Lesson 1

- We live on the planet called Earth.
- Earth is part of a solar system.
- There are eight planets in our solar system.
- There are also asteroids and comets in our solar system.
- The planets, asteroids, and comets orbit, or move around, the sun.
- Our solar system is part of the Milky Way galaxy.

### Lesson 2

- There are billions of stars in each galaxy.
- There are billions of galaxies in the universe.
- Some stars make patterns that we call constellations.
- A star's color tells us how hot it is.
- Scientists group stars by temperature, brightness, and size.
- Each star has a life cycle.

### Get Ready

Earth is the planet we live on. Can you name any other planets? Look at the picture below. Write the planet names. _____

_____

_____

_____

_____

_____

_____

_____

## Vocabulary

◄ This is an illustration of our **solar system**. Earth and seven other planets **orbit**, or move around, the sun.

Earth has an **atmosphere** around it. The atmosphere is made of gases. ▼

▲ This is a **galaxy**. A galaxy is a group of stars, planets, gases, and dust. Dust is tiny pieces of dirt.

Key Words

asteroids

atmosphere

comet

galaxy

orbit

solar system

▲ **Asteroids** are pieces of rock and metal. They orbit the sun.

▲ This ball of ice and dust is a **comet**. Comets also orbit the sun.

## Practice

Choose the word that correctly completes each sentence.

1. _____ are pieces of rock and metal that orbit the sun.

   **a.** Asteroids  **b.** Atmospheres  **c.** Galaxies

2. Earth and seven other planets _____ the sun.

   **a.** solar system  **b.** comet  **c.** orbit

3. Earth has an _____ of gases around it.

   **a.** orbit  **b.** atmosphere  **c.** asteroids

4. Eight planets and the sun are in our _____.

   **a.** solar system  **b.** comet  **c.** atmosphere

5. A _____ is a group of stars, planets, gases, and dust.

   **a.** comet  **b.** galaxy  **c.** orbit

6. A _____ is a ball of ice and dust.

   **a.** asteroids  **b.** solar system  **c.** comet

For more practice, go to page 113.

# Science Skills

## Science Reading Strategy: **Reread**

When a paragraph is difficult, **reread** it.

- Read the paragraph once to understand the most important ideas.
- Read the paragraph again to understand more details.

Read the text below once. Then cover it. Answer question 1. Then reread the text and answer the other questions.

The large dark areas you see on the moon are called maria (MAH-ree-uh). *Maria* is a Latin word meaning "seas." Scientists thought that there were large areas of water on the moon. Actually, the maria are areas of rock. The rock was once liquid. The maria came from volcanoes on the moon's surface.

◀ The dark areas on the moon are maria.

1. What are the large dark areas you see on the moon?

2. Why are they called maria?

3. Where did the maria come from?

Look for an **As You Read** question in the lesson. It will ask you to reread. It will help you understand the lesson.

For more practice, go to page 114.

## Using Visuals: **Illustrations**

An illustration is a drawing or a painting. Illustrations are useful in science
books. Some things are not easy to photograph. An artist can create a
picture of these things instead.

Look at the illustration. Then answer the questions.

◄ Illustration of Venus
without its atmosphere

1.  Turn to page 104 to see a photo of Venus. How is the
    photo different from the illustration?

2.  Why can't scientists take a photo of Venus without
    its atmosphere?

3.  How does Venus's surface look in the illustration?

**For more practice, go to pages 115–116.**

# The Solar System

Look up at the sky on a clear night. What do you see? The moon. Stars. Planets.

You may not know the names of the stars and planets you see. But you can be sure of one thing. Every object you see in the sky is part of the Milky Way galaxy.

A galaxy is a group of stars, planets, gases, and dust. Earth, the planet we live on, is part of the Milky Way galaxy.

▲ Our solar system is part of the Milky Way.

▼ All the stars you see are in the Milky Way galaxy.

There are many galaxies in space. Each galaxy has many solar systems. A solar system is a group of objects that orbit a star.

Our solar system is made up of Earth, seven other planets, and the sun. The planets orbit the sun. Our sun is a star.

Like all stars, the sun is a ball of hot, glowing gases. It has a strong pulling force called gravity. The sun's gravity keeps each planet moving in its path, or orbit. The shape of the orbits is more **oval** than round.

---

**oval:** shaped like an egg

▲ Our solar system

## Before You Go On

1. What is a galaxy?
2. What is a solar system?
3. Why can't you see stars in other galaxies?

# The Inner Planets

The first four planets are Mercury, Venus, Earth, and Mars. They are called the inner planets. They are closer to the sun than the other planets. They are made mostly of rock.

Mercury is closest to the sun. The sun's heat makes the planet hot and dry. It is covered with holes called craters. Mercury is small—about one-third the size of Earth.

Venus is hotter than Mercury. This is because of Venus's atmosphere. Clouds of **poisonous** gases cover the planet. The thick clouds trap the heat.

---

**poisonous:** containing substances that harm or kill living things

**LANGUAGE TIP**

**close**
**closer**
**closest**

*Earth is* close *to the sun.*

*Venus is* closer *to the sun.*

*Mercury is* closest *to the sun.*

▲ Venus

◀ Mercury

Earth is the only planet that we know has life. Earth's atmosphere contains oxygen. Animals need oxygen to live.

Earth is also the only planet with liquid water. Water covers more than 70 percent of Earth's surface. That's why people sometimes call Earth the blue planet.

Mars is farther from the sun than Earth. So Mars is colder than Earth. Mars has a reddish, rocky surface. It is often called the red planet.

## SCIENCE ═NOW═

**Robots on Mars**

Scientists put robots called rovers on Mars. The rovers take pictures of the planet's surface. We are learning a lot about Mars from these pictures. For example, scientists now think that there was once water on Mars.

▲ Illustration of a rover on Mars

▲ Earth

Mars ▶

## Before You Go On

1. Name the inner planets.
2. Which planet is the hottest? Why?
3. How is the atmosphere on Earth different from the one on Venus?

# The Outer Planets

Jupiter, Saturn, Uranus, and Neptune are the outer planets. They are far from the sun and very cold. The outer planets are made mostly of gases. Like clouds, the gases look solid from far away.

Jupiter is the largest planet in the solar system. It is about eleven times the size of Earth. Its atmosphere is very windy. The red spot on its surface is a giant windstorm. Jupiter has rings, but they are hard to see.

Saturn is the second largest planet. It has bright rings that are easy to see. The rings are made of pieces of rock and ice that orbit the planet.

▲ Jupiter

▲ Saturn

Uranus is the seventh planet from the sun. It is less than half the size of Saturn. But it is four times the size of Earth. Uranus has thin, dark rings.

Neptune, the next planet, is about the same size as Uranus. Like Jupiter, Neptune has a windy atmosphere. Storms there can last hundreds of years.

Pluto, once considered a planet, was renamed a "dwarf planet" in 2006, when scientists changed the definition of *planet*. Pluto no longer fits the definition of *planet* because of its small size, among other things.

**LANGUAGE TIP**

four ⟶ fourth

seven ⟶ seventh

## As You Read

**Reread**

Read the first paragraph. Now answer this question: *How big is the planet Uranus?* Reread the paragraph to find the answer.

▲ Uranus

▲ Neptune

▲ Pluto, the "dwarf planet"

### Before You Go On

1. What are most of the outer planets made of?
2. Which planet is colder, Jupiter or Neptune? Why?
3. Why is Pluto no longer called a "planet"?

# Asteroids and Comets

Asteroids and comets are also part of our solar system. Asteroids **consist of** pieces of rock and metal. They can be very small or hundreds of kilometers wide. Most of the asteroids in our solar system orbit the sun between Mars and Jupiter.

Comets also orbit the sun. A comet is a huge mass of ice, frozen gases, and dust. You can see a comet when it is near the sun. The sun heats up the comet. This causes the ice to turn into a cloud of gases with a long tail. Comets do not make their own light. Like mirrors, comets **reflect** the sun's light.

---

**consist of:** made up or composed of
**reflect:** throw or bend back

▼ Comet Hale-Bopp

## SCIENCE AT HOME

**Watching for Comets**

How do you know when to look for a comet? The brightest comets can be seen only every ten to twelve years. A comet is big news. So you may hear about it on TV or read about it in the newspaper. You can also use the Internet to find out more about when to see comets.

# Exploring

## An Asteroid Changes Earth

A big asteroid fell to Earth 65 million years ago. It hit in what is now Mexico. The asteroid was about 10 kilometers wide. The asteroid was moving so fast that it made a hole almost 200 kilometers wide.

The asteroid crash changed Earth. It caused an explosion that started huge fires. The dust and smoke made a dark cloud. No sunlight reached Earth for months. Many kinds of plants and animals died. Some scientists think that this asteroid killed the dinosaurs.

▼ Illustration of an asteroid hitting Earth

## Before You Go On

1. What is an asteroid?
2. Where are most of the asteroids in our solar system?
3. How are asteroids and comets the same? How are they different?

## Vocabulary

Complete each sentence with the correct word or phrase.

| | | |
|---|---|---|
| asteroids | galaxy | comet |
| orbit | atmosphere | solar system |

1. Venus has an _____ of poisonous gases.

2. A _____ is a group of stars, planets, gases, and dust.

3. Planets, asteroids, and comets all _____ the sun.

4. Pieces of rock and metal that orbit the sun are called _____.

5. A _____ is a huge mass of ice, frozen gases, and dust.

6. Earth and seven other planets are all part of our _____.

## Check Your Understanding

Write the answer to each question.

1. Which two planets are the hottest? _____

2. What are the four inner planets mostly made of? _____

3. What are the four outer planets mostly made of? _____

4. What is Pluto? _____

## Apply Science Skills

### Science Reading Strategy: **Reread**

Write the answer to each question in your notebook. If you can't answer all of the questions, reread page 109.

1. When did a big asteroid fall to Earth?

2. Where did it hit?

3. How long did Earth go without sunlight?

4. What do scientists think this asteroid killed?

## Using Visuals: **Illustrations**

This illustration shows the dwarf planet, Pluto, and its moon, Charon.

Look at the illustration. Then answer the questions.

▼ Illustration of Pluto and its moon

1. Compare the photo of Pluto on page 107 with this illustration. How are they different?

2. What do you think the yellow light in the upper left corner is?

3. How would you describe Pluto, as shown in this illustration?

# Discuss

Why can't people live on Mercury or Venus? Why can't people live on the outer planets?

# Practice Pages

PRACTICE

# Before You Read

## VOCABULARY

**A.** Draw an arrow from each key word to its definition.

| | |
|---|---|
| **1.** solar system | ball of ice and dust |
| **2.** atmosphere | a group of stars, planets, gases, and dust |
| **3.** galaxy | eight planets orbiting the sun |
| **4.** asteroids | move around the sun |
| **5.** comet | made of gases |
| **6.** orbit | pieces of rock and metal |

**B.** Write four sentences below using a key word and its definition.

**1.** _____

**2.** _____

**3.** _____

**4.** _____

**C.** Circle the best word to complete each sentence.

**1.** The Earth (orbits / gases) the sun.

**2.** A galaxy is a group of planets, (oxygen / stars), gases, and dust.

**3.** The atmosphere is made of (metals / gases).

**4.** A comet is a ball of dust and (stars / ice).

**5.** (Galaxies / Asteroids) are pieces of metal and rock.

**D.** Write T for *true* or F for *false.* Correct the sentences that are false.

_____ **1.** Galaxies orbit the sun.

_____ **2.** A comet is a ball of ice and dust.

_____ **3.** Gases make up a planet's atmosphere.

_____ **4.** Asteroids are groups of stars and planets.

_____ **5.** A solar system is a group of planets orbiting a sun.

## Science Reading Strategy: Reread

**A.** Read the paragraph below. Then cover the paragraph. Answer question 1.

      The planet we live on is called Earth. Earth's atmosphere is made up of several gases. One of these gases is oxygen. People and other animals need oxygen to survive. Earth is just one of eight planets in our solar system. All the planets in our solar system orbit a bright star—the sun. Asteroids and comets are part of our solar system, too. They also orbit the sun.

**1.** What is Earth's atmosphere made up of?

_____

**B.** Reread the paragraph and answer the questions.

**2.** What important gas is part of Earth's atmosphere?

_____

**3.** What is Earth part of?

_____

**4.** How many planets are there in our solar system?

_____

**5.** What orbits the sun?

_____

**C.** Reread the paragraph again. Write three sentences about Earth.

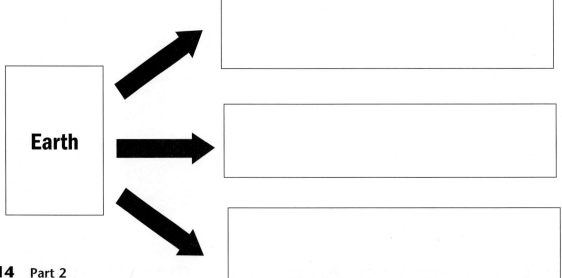

PRACTICE

## Using Visuals: Illustrations

**A.** Look at the illustration of our solar system. Read the paragraph. Then answer the questions.

> Illustrations are good tools for teaching about stars and planets. It isn't easy to take pictures of the planets in our solar system. Scientists have to use big telescopes with a special camera. The planets in our solar system are so far away from one another that even scientists cannot include them all in the same photo. But an artist can look at photos of each planet and use them as models. Then the artist draws or paints the eight planets together, as they appear in the solar system.

1. How do scientists take photographs of the planets in our solar system?

   _____

2. Why can't scientists include all eight planets in the same photo?

   _____

3. How can an artist use photos?

   _____

4. How many planets can you see in this illustration?

   _____

5. Name the planets, moving from left to right.

   _____

**B.** Look at the picture. Choose the best answer. Circle the letter.

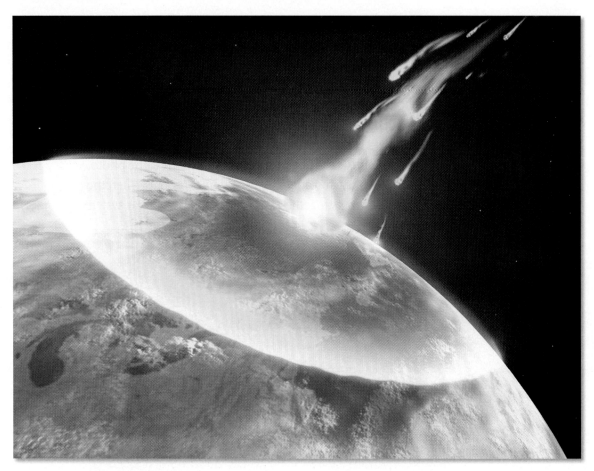

1. This picture is _____.

   **a.** a photograph      **b.** a diagram      **c.** an illustration

2. This picture shows _____.

   **a.** a comet orbiting the sun      **b.** an asteroid hitting a planet      **c.** a volcano erupting on Mars

3. This event caused _____.

   **a.** fires      **b.** floods      **c.** ice storms

4. The planet in this picture is _____.

   **a.** Earth      **b.** Mars      **c.** Pluto

5. The event shown in this picture _____.

   **a.** never happened      **b.** happened recently      **c.** happened a long time ago

# Lesson 1 Review

## VOCABULARY

Complete the puzzle. Use key words. Write the secret word.

1.  The Milky Way is a _____.  ⬭ __ __ __ __ __

2.  _____ are made up of rock and metal.  ⬭ __ __ __ __ __ __ __ __

3.  Earth has a(n) _____ around it.  __ __ __ __ ⬭ __ __ __ __

4.  A _____ is a ball of ice and dust.  __ __ __ ⬭ __

5.  Our _____ has eight planets.  ⬭ __ __ __ __    __ __ __ __ __

**Secret word:** __ __ __ __ __

## VOCABULARY IN CONTEXT

Complete the paragraph. Use words from the box.

| comets | galaxy | asteroids | solar system | atmosphere |
|---|---|---|---|---|

    Our **(1)** _____ is made up of eight planets with a sun in the center.

It belongs to a **(2)** _____ called the Milky Way. **(3)** _____

and **(4)** _____ are also part of our solar system. Earth is the only

planet whose **(5)** _____ contains oxygen.

## CHECK YOUR UNDERSTANDING

Answer the questions.

1.  In what galaxy do we live?

_____

2.  What do you call the path that each planet moves in?

_____

3.  What are the four planets closest to the sun?

_____

4.  What are the four planets farthest from the sun?

_____

## Science Reading Strategy: Reread

Answer the questions. If you can't answer them all, reread page 108.

**1.** What are asteroids?

_____

**2.** Where do asteroids in our solar system orbit the sun?

_____

**3.** What are comets made of?

_____

**4.** What happens when the sun heats up a comet?

_____

**5.** Do comets reflect light from the sun or do they make their own light?

_____

## Using Visuals: Illustrations

Look at the illustration. Then answer the questions.

**1.** What does this illustration show? _____

**2.** What planets do you see? _____

**3.** To which solar system do these planets belong? _____

**4.** In what ways is this illustration not realistic? _____

_____

# Science Journal

Write about five interesting things you have learned in this lesson.

1. _____

   _____

   _____

2. _____

   _____

   _____

3. _____

   _____

   _____

4. _____

   _____

   _____

5. _____

   _____

   _____

## Vocabulary

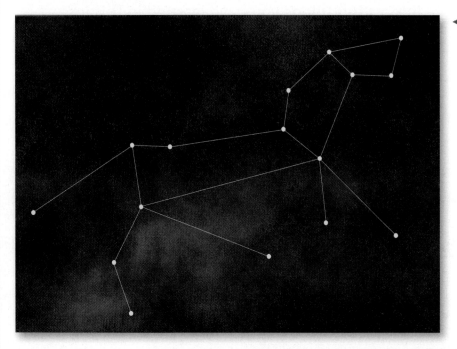

◄ A **constellation** is a group of stars that make a pattern. This constellation is Leo the lion.

This is a **telescope**. Scientists called **astronomers** use telescopes to see other planets, stars, and galaxies. ►

The **universe** is everything in space. There are many galaxies in the universe, including many trillions of stars. A **trillion** is the number 1,000,000,000,000. ▼

**Key Words**

**astronomers**

**constellation**

**telescope**

**trillion**

**universe**

## Practice

Next to each word, write its meaning. Use your own words.

1. astronomers _scientists who study other galaxies, planets, and stars_

2. constellation_____

3. telescope _____

4. trillion_____

5. universe_____

For more practice, go to page 135.

# Science Skills

## Science Reading Strategy: **Visualize**

When you read you can **visualize,** or make pictures of the words in your mind.

Read the text below. As you read, visualize the words.

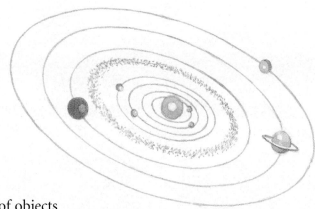

Our solar system is a group of objects in space. In the center is the sun. Earth and seven other planets circle around the sun. Each planet has its own pathway, called an orbit. The orbits are almost round. They are shaped like squashed circles.

1. What does our solar system look like?

2. Describe the shape of the planets' orbits.

3. Which words in the text helped you visualize the solar system?

Look for an **As You Read** question in the lesson. It will help you understand the lesson.

For more practice, go to pages 136–137.

## Using Visuals: **Deep Space Photos**

NASA's Hubble Space Telescope took this photograph of deep space.
The photo shows thousands of stars of different colors. A star's color tells
how hot it is. Below the photo, a color key shows which colors are hotter
and which are cooler.

    Look at the photo. Then discuss the questions.

Hubble Space Telescope ▶

coolest                                                              hottest

1.  What color are the hottest stars? What color are the coolest stars?

2.  List the colors in the color key from coolest to hottest.

3.  Do you see a star of each color in the photo? Point to them.

For more practice, go to page 138.

# Lesson 2

# Beyond the Solar System

To us, our solar system seems huge. But it is a very small part of space. There are many billions of stars in the Milky Way galaxy. Our sun is just one of these stars.

There are also many billions of galaxies in the universe. *Universe* is a name for everything in space, including planets, stars, and galaxies.

▲ Photos of the planets in our solar system

▲ Illustration of Milky Way

How many stars are there in the universe? There are so many that it's hard to imagine—perhaps a trillion trillion. That number is a 1 followed by twenty-four zeros. There are more stars in the universe than there are grains of sand on all the beaches of Earth.

▲ This photo of deep space was taken using the Hubble Space Telescope. The shapes you see are different galaxies.

## Before You Go On

1. What is the universe?
2. How many stars are there in the universe?
3. How is the photo above different from what you see in the sky at night?

# Constellations

The stars we know best are the ones closest to us. Some of these stars make patterns that look like people or animals. We call these star patterns constellations.

One of the best-known star patterns is the Big Dipper. A dipper is a cup with a long handle. The Big Dipper is not a true constellation. It is part of a constellation called Ursa Major, the Great Bear. The Big Dipper's handle is also the bear's tail.

◄ Ursa Major, the Great Bear

▼ Big Dipper

Another well-known constellation is Orion. Orion is a person in a myth, or story, from **ancient** Greece. He was a great hunter. On a clear night, look for the three stars that make his belt. Once you have found his belt, it is easy to see his right thigh and his shoulders.

---

**ancient:** very old

▲ Most of the stars that make up the constellation Orion

◀ The constellation Orion

## SCIENCE AT HOME

**Antares and Scorpio**

On a clear night, look for a bright red star. From the northern part of Earth, it can be seen low in the sky. From the southern part, it will be high in the sky. This star is Antares (an-TAIR-eez). It is the heart of the constellation Scorpio. In the Greek myth, Scorpio kills Orion. In the sky, Orion looks like he is running away from Scorpio.

Antares

### Before You Go On

1. What is a constellation?
2. What is the Big Dipper?
3. Why do you think people made up myths about the stars?

# Star Facts

Look at the sky during the daytime. Do you see any stars? Sure. You see the sun. But there are other stars, too. Why can't you see them? Because the sun's brightness overpowers the brightness of other stars.

The brightest star in the night sky is a star called Sirius. It is larger, hotter, and brighter than the sun. But from Earth, the sun looks brighter than Sirius. That's because the sun is much closer to us. What if the sun and Sirius were the same distance from Earth? Then you could see how much brighter Sirius really is.

▲ The brightest star in this photo is Sirius.

## LANGUAGE TIP

**bright** —→ adjective

**brightness** —→ noun

*Look at that* bright *star.*

*Look at the* brightness *of that star.*

## ENVIRONMENT WATCH

### Light Pollution

On a dark night, you might see about 2,500 stars. But in cities you might be able to see only a few hundred. Why? City lights make it hard to see the night sky. This is called light pollution. Changing the type of lightbulbs in streetlights can help. It can also lower costs and save energy.

▲ Bright city lights make it hard to see stars.

The color of a star tells you how hot it is. Blue stars are the hottest. Then come white stars. Sirius is a blue-white star. Yellow stars, like the sun, are medium hot. Orange stars are cooler. Red stars are the coolest.

Stars come in all different sizes. The sun is a medium-sized star. Many stars are smaller than the sun. Stars called giants are much larger than the sun.

▲ What different colors of stars can you see?

## Before You Go On

1. Why can't you see stars other than the sun during the daytime?
2. Why does the sun look brighter than Sirius?
3. Which star is hotter, Sirius or the sun? How do you know?

A star has a life cycle. It begins as a cloud of gases and dust. Then the gases and dust pull together. They begin to glow and get very hot. The new star releases heat and light.

In time, the star uses up most of its **fuel**. Then it begins to expand, or get bigger. Finally the star becomes so big that it cannot hold onto its outer layers. These gases form rings around the dying star. The star ends its life in a cloud of gases.

---

**fuel:** something that burns to give heat or light

## As You Read

**Visualize**

Which words help you visualize the life cycle of a star?

▼ **Stars form in clouds like this.**

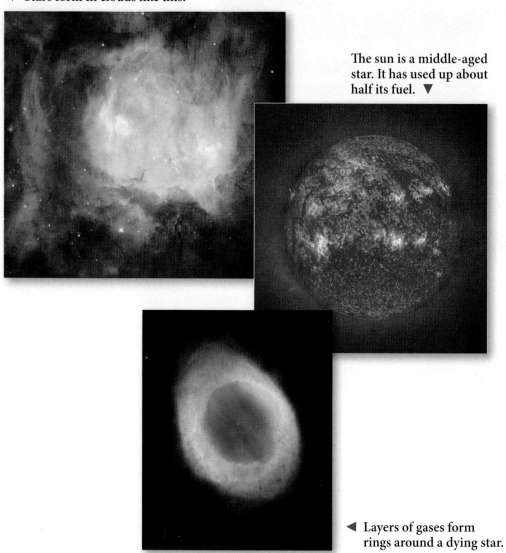

The sun is a middle-aged star. It has used up about half its fuel. ▼

◀ Layers of gases form rings around a dying star.

## Leaders in Science

### Edwin Hubble (1889–1953)

Edwin Hubble was an astronomer—a scientist who studies objects in space. Hubble saw that galaxies were moving away from Earth. He guessed that the universe is getting bigger. The Hubble Space Telescope is named for him. This telescope orbits Earth and takes pictures.

▲ Edwin Hubble

Hubble Space Telescope ▶

With the Hubble Space Telescope, astronomers can see many different galaxies. Galaxies have two main shapes: spiral and elliptical.

◀ Elliptical galaxy

▲ Spiral galaxy

### Before You Go On

1. How does a star begin its life?

2. What are the two main shapes of galaxies?

3. How did the Hubble Space Telescope help us learn about the universe?

## Vocabulary

Complete each sentence with a word from the box.

| | |
|---|---|
| constellation | universe |
| Telescope | astronomer |

1. The Hubble Space _____ takes pictures of faraway stars and galaxies.

2. Orion is a _____ .

3. The _____ is everything in space.

4. An _____ is a person who studies objects in space.

## Check Your Understanding

Write the answer to each question.

1. How does a star end its life? _____

2. What are constellations? _____

3. What are the hottest and coolest colors of stars? _____

4. Why don't other stars look as bright as the sun? _____

## Apply Science Skills

### Science Reading Strategy: Visualize

Read the paragraph and visualize what you read. Draw a picture of what you see.

**Two Very Different Sisters**

Venus and Earth are like sisters in some ways. They are about the same size and made of similar materials. They are next to each other in the solar system. But Venus is very different from Earth. Venus has no water. It is covered by thick clouds of poisonous gases. The thick clouds trap the sun's heat. How hot is it on Venus? So hot that you could bake a cake in a few seconds—without an oven!

## Using Visuals: **Deep Space Photos**

The Hubble Space Telescope took these photographs of deep space.
The photo on the left shows thousands of galaxies in deep space. The
photo on the right shows a close-up of one section.

Look at the close-up. Then answer the questions.

1.  Can you find a spiral galaxy? Point to it.

2.  Can you find an elliptical galaxy? Point to it.

## Discuss

There are many billions of galaxies in the universe. One
galaxy can have many millions of solar systems. Do you
think there are any other planets like Earth out in space?
What does a planet need to support the kinds of life we
have on Earth?

**For more practice, go to pages 139–140.**

# Practice Pages

PRACTICE

# Before You Read

## VOCABULARY

**A.** Draw an arrow from each key word to its definition.

| | |
|---|---|
| **1.** constellation | everything in space |
| **2.** telescope | a star pattern |
| **3.** astronomers | a tool people use to see objects in space |
| **4.** universe | a very large number |
| **5.** trillion | scientists who study objects in space |

**B.** Write five sentences using each key word and its definition.

**1.** _____

**2.** _____

**3.** _____

**4.** _____

**5.** _____

**C.** Write T for *true* or F for *false*. Correct the sentences that are false.

_____ **1.** Astronomers study rocks and minerals.

_____ **2.** Constellations are groups of stars that form patterns.

_____ **3.** The universe is everything in space.

_____ **4.** A telescope is a planet seen by astronomers.

_____ **5.** A trillion is a kind of asteroid.

**D.** Match the parts of the sentence. Write the letter.

_____ **1.** Leo the lion is a      **a.** number.

_____ **2.** Our solar system is part of the      **b.** scientists.

_____ **3.** Astronomers are      **c.** constellation.

_____ **4.** A telescope is used to observe      **d.** universe.

_____ **5.** A trillion is a very big      **e.** planets, stars, and galaxies.

**PRACTICE**

## Science Reading Strategy: Visualize

**A.** Read the paragraph below. As you read, visualize the universe.

The universe is everything in space. Space is a very dark place filled with stars, planets, comets, and galaxies. The stars can be different colors: red, orange, yellow, white, or blue. The Milky Way galaxy is the home of our solar system. It has a spiral shape. At the center is a ball. Coming out from the ball are long groups of stars called arms. The arms are curved because the whole galaxy is spinning.

**B.** Make a picture of how you visualized the universe.

PRACTICE

# Science Reading Strategy: Visualize

Read the paragraph below. Visualize the stages in the life cycle of a star. Illustrate the stages in the boxes provided.

The stars in the universe do not live forever. Each star has a life cycle. It begins its life as a cloud of gases and dust. The gases and dust pull together. The cloud gets smaller, brighter, and hotter. Soon a new star is born. It is hot and bright, like our sun. In time, the star uses up most of its fuel. Then the star gets bigger, redder, and cooler. Finally the star gets so huge that it cannot hold onto its outer layers of gases. These gases form rings around the dying star. The star ends its life in a cloud of gases.

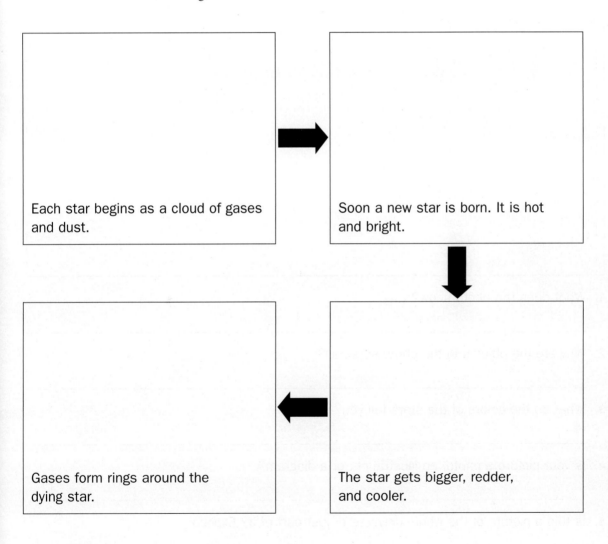

Each star begins as a cloud of gases and dust.

Soon a new star is born. It is hot and bright.

Gases form rings around the dying star.

The star gets bigger, redder, and cooler.

PRACTICE

## Using Visuals: Deep Space Photos

In the space below, draw a picture of the deep space photo on page 123.
Use the same colors as the photo. Then answer the questions.

1. What does the photo show?

_____

2. Why are the objects in the photo so small?

_____

3. What do the colors of the stars tell you?

_____

4. Is your picture a photo, an illustration, or a diagram?

_____

5. Is this a picture of the whole universe or just part of it? Explain.

_____

# Lesson 2 Review

## VOCABULARY

Use the words in the box to identify each clue. Write the word on the line.

| constellation | trillion | astronomer | telescope | universe |

**1.** I am a scientist who studies objects in space. _____

**2.** I have galaxies, stars, and planets in me. _____

**3.** I am a tool used to observe objects in space. _____

**4.** I am a very large number. _____

**5.** I am a group of stars that makes a pattern. _____

## VOCABULARY IN CONTEXT

Write T for *true* or F for *false*. Correct the sentences that are false.

_____ **1.** An astronomer studies plants.

_____ **2.** The Hubble is a telescope in space.

_____ **3.** A constellation is a group of solar systems.

_____ **4.** There are many stars and planets in the universe.

## CHECK YOUR UNDERSTANDING

Choose the best answer. Circle the letter.

**1.** A blue star is _____.

    **a.** very far away    **b.** very hot        **c.** very cool

**2.** There are two kinds of galaxies: spiral and _____.

    **a.** constellation    **b.** elliptical      **c.** Milky Way

**3.** Orion and Ursa Major are _____.

    **a.** cool stars      **b.** comets       **c.** constellations

**4.** _____ is everything in space, including galaxies and planets.

    **a.** The universe    **b.** A trillion     **c.** A comet

## Science Reading Strategy: Visualize

Read the paragraph below. Visualize what the paragraph describes about Earth. Then draw what you visualize.

> The planet we live on is called Earth. Earth is an important part of our solar system. It is often called the blue planet because water covers more than 70 percent of Earth's surface. Our solar system is made up of Earth and seven more planets orbiting a bright star—our sun. It is the third planet from the sun.

## Using Visuals: Deep Space Photos

Look at the deep space photo of the universe on page 125. Then answer the questions below.

**1.** What do you see in the photo? _____

**2.** What different shapes of galaxies do you see? _____

**3.** What different colors do you see? _____

**4.** How can you tell that it is a deep space photo? _____

**140**　Part 2

PRACTICE

# Science Journal

Write about five interesting things you have learned in this lesson.

1. _____
   _____
   _____

2. _____
   _____
   _____

3. _____
   _____
   _____

4. _____
   _____
   _____

5. _____
   _____
   _____

# Part Review

## Vocabulary

Answer the questions with words or phrases from the box.

| | | | |
|---|---|---|---|
| constellation | solar system | comet | galaxy |
| astronomer | orbit | atmosphere | telescope |
| asteroids | universe | trillion | |

1. What is the Milky Way? _____

_____

2. What is everything in space? _____

_____

3. What is the layer of gases around Earth? _____

_____

4. What do Earth, seven other planets, and the sun make up? _____

_____

5. What is a planet's path around the sun called? _____

_____

6. What is a person who studies objects in space called? _____

_____

7. What are pieces of rock and metal in space? _____

_____

8. What is made of ice and dust and has a tail? _____

_____

9. What is the number 1,000,000,000,000? _____

_____

10. What is Ursa Major? _____

_____

11. What do scientists use to see other planets, stars, and galaxies? _____

_____

# Check Your Understanding

Write T for *true* or F for *false*. Then rewrite each false statement to make it correct.

_____ 1. Earth is the only planet in our solar system with oxygen and liquid water.

_____ 2. The four inner planets are made mostly of gases.

_____ 3. The outer planets are made mostly of rock.

_____ 4. There are trillions of stars in the universe.

_____ 5. Red stars are hotter than blue stars.

_____ 6. The two main shapes of galaxies are spiral and elliptical.

# Extension Project

Work with a partner to make a poster about one of the planets in the solar system. Include a drawing and interesting facts about the planet.

# Apply Science Skills

## Using Visuals: Deep Space Photos

This photograph was taken using the Hubble Space Telescope. It shows a dying star. Look at the photo. Then answer the questions.

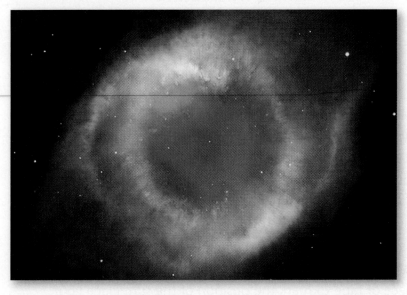

◄ Our sun will probably look something like this when it dies.

1. How is this star like the dying star shown on page 130?

2. What are the rings made of?

# Part Experiment

## How Big Is the Solar System?

In this activity, you will make scale models of the planets. This will show you how different the sizes of the planets are. Then you will make a scale model of the solar system. This will show you how far each planet is from the sun.

## Purpose

To make a scale model of the solar system

## Materials

metric ruler
metric tape measure
compass
construction paper
markers, colored pencils
scissors
tape

◄ Drawing a circle
with a compass

## What to Do

1.  The third column of the Data Table on the next page lists the scale sizes of the sun and each planet. Use these sizes to make your models. For example, Jupiter's diameter will be 14.3 centimeters. On construction paper, measure 14.3 centimeters and draw a line of that length. Then use a compass to draw a circle of that diameter. To do this, place the point of the compass at the center of the line before you draw your circle. Then cut out the circle. Use colored pencils or markers to draw special features such as Jupiter's red spot. Do this for each planet and the sun.

2.  The fifth column of the Data Table lists each planet's scale distance from the sun. Use these distances to make your solar system model. In a large room or hallway, use a piece of tape to mark the position of the sun. Place your sun model at this point. Then measure the scale distance for each planet. Place your model for each planet at the correct distance.

## Data Table

| Solar System Body | Diameter | | Distance from Sun | |
| | Actual Size (kilometers) | Scale Size (centimeters) | Actual Distance (millions of kilometers) | Scale Distance (centimeters) |
| --- | --- | --- | --- | --- |
| Sun | 1,400,000 | 140 (1.4 m) | — | — |
| Mercury | 4,878 | .5 | 58 | 5.8 |
| Venus | 12,104 | 1.2 | 108 | 10.8 |
| Earth | 12,756 | 1.3 | 150 | 15 |
| Mars | 6,794 | .7 | 228 | 22.8 |
| Jupiter | 142,800 | 14.3 | 778 | 77.8 |
| Saturn | 120,540 | 12 | 1,427 | 142.7 |
| Uranus | 51,200 | 5.1 | 2,871 | 287 |
| Neptune | 49,500 | 4.9 | 4,497 | 449 |

## Draw Conclusions

Work with a partner. Discuss your conclusions. Then write them under Step 5 on page 146.

1. How do the sizes of the planets compare to one another? How do the sizes of the planets compare to the size of the sun?

2. Why did you have to use different scales for the sizes of the planets and their distances from the sun?

# Experiment Log:
# How Big Is the Solar System?

Follow the steps of the scientific method as you do your experiment. Write notes about each step as the experiment progresses.

**Step 1: Ask questions.**

**Step 2: Make a hypothesis.**

**Step 3: Test your hypothesis.**

**Step 4: Observe.**

**Step 5: Draw conclusions.**

# Write About It

1. Think about these objects in space: comets, stars, planets, and asteroids. Which object is the most interesting to you? Write a paragraph about it.

2. Scientists have discovered ice on Mars. Some say that where there is water, there is life. Do you agree? Do you think there is or ever was life on Mars? Write a paragraph explaining why or why not.

# Glossary

## Phonetic Respelling Key

| | | | | |
|---|---|---|---|---|
| a | cat | o | stop | |
| ah | father | oh | go, slow, toe | |
| air | hair, there, their | oo | moon, blue, do | |
| ar | arm | yoo | you, music, few | |
| ay | play, make, eight, they | or | for, your | |
| aw | draw, all, walk | oi | soil, boy | |
| e | red, said | ow | brown, out | |
| ee | green, please, she | u | put, look | |
| eer | ear, here | uh | but, what, from, about, seven | |
| eye | like, right, fly | er | her, work, bird, fur | |
| i | six | | | |

**ancient** (AYN-shuhnt)
Very old.

**ash** (ash)
Gray powder that is left after something is burned.

**ask questions** (ask KWES-chuhnz)
**1.** A reading strategy. Ask yourself questions about the text. This helps you check your understanding. **2.** Step 1 of the scientific method. The purpose of an experiment is to find out answers to the questions asked in step 1.

**asteroids** (AS-tuh-roidz)
Pieces of rock and metal that orbit, or circle around, the sun.

**astronomers** (uh-STRAHN-uh-merz)
People who study stars, planets, and other objects in space.

**atmosphere** (AT-muhs-feer)
The gases above the surface of a planet. Earth's atmosphere contains oxygen.

**cause and effect** (kawz and uh-FEKT)
A reading strategy. Looking for cause and effect can help you understand a text better. A cause makes something happen. The effect is what happens.

**chart** (chart)
A kind of visual. A chart often shows information in columns and rows.

**comet** (KOM-uht)
A big mass of ice, frozen gases, and dust that orbits, or circles, the sun. A comet often has a bright tail.

**consist of** (kuhn-SIST of)
Made up of or composed of.

**constellation** (kahn-stuh-LAY-shuhn)
A group of stars that make a pattern in the sky. The Great Bear and Orion are examples of constellations.

**crust** (krust)
First layer of the Earth. One of Earth's four layers.

**crystals** (KRIS-tlz)
Shapes that repeat and are all the same in a mineral, rock, or other solid.

**cycle diagram** (SEYE-kuhl DEYE-uh-gram)
A kind of visual. A cycle diagram is a labeled drawing, often in the shape of a circle. It shows events that happen again and again in the same order.

**deep space photo** (deep spays FOH-toh)
A kind of visual. A photograph of stars and galaxies far from Earth is called a deep space photo.

**diagram** (DEYE-uh-gram)
A kind of visual. A diagram is a drawing with labels, or words. The labels tell what the picture is showing.

**draw conclusions**
(draw kuhn-KLOO-zhuhnz)
Step 5 of the scientific method. You draw conclusions at the end of an experiment. You decide whether your hypothesis is correct.

**earthquake** (ERTH-kwayk)
A sudden shaking of the ground. This happens when the Earth's crust moves.

**elliptical** (uh-LIP-tuh-kuhl)
Stretched out; one of the two main shapes a galaxy can be.

**erosion** (uh-ROH-zhuhn)
The wearing down and moving of rocks and soil caused by water, ice, and wind.

**fossils** (FOS-uhlz)
Parts of plants or animals that turned into rock over time.

**fuel** (FYOO-uhl)
Something that burns to give heat or light.

**galaxy** (GAL-uhk-see)
A group of stars, planets, gases, and dust. Our sun and Earth are part of the Milky Way galaxy. There are many billions of galaxies in space.

**geologist** (jee-OL-uh-juhst)
A person who studies geology.

**geology** (jee-OL-uh-jee)
The study of rocks and minerals. Geology also includes the study of the changing shape of the Earth's surface.

**glacier** (GLAY-sher)
A very big sheet of ice. A glacier can move rocks and soil.

**igneous** (IG-nee-yuhs)
The kind of rock that forms when hot liquid rock cools and hardens. Igneous rock forms above and under the ground.

**illustration** (il-uhs-TRAY-shuhn)
A kind of visual. An illustration is a drawing or a painting.

**inner core** (IN-er kor)
Fourth and innermost level of the Earth's four layers. It is made of solid metal.

**inner planets (IN-er PLAN-itz)**
The first four planets that are closest to the sun. They are made mostly of rock. Mercury, Venus, Earth, and Mars are the inner planets.

**lichens (LEYE-kuhnz)**
Plantlike things that produce chemicals. These chemicals can cause rock to break apart.

**make a hypothesis**
**(mayk uh heye-PAH-thuh-suhs)**
Step 2 of the scientific method. A hypothesis is a guess. You guess what the experiment will show. Then you do the experiment to see if your hypothesis is correct.

**mantle (MAN-tuhl)**
Second layer of the Earth's four layers. It is made of hot, soft rock.

**maria (muh-REE-uh)**
Areas of rock on the moon.

**measure (MEZH-uhr)**
To find out facts about something by using standard tools. Different tools measure different things. For example, a ruler measures length, or how long something is. A balance measures mass. Special containers measure volume.

**metamorphic (met-uh-MOR-fik)**
The kind of rock that forms when igneous or sedimentary rock is changed by great heat and pressure. Marble is a metamorphic rock.

**micrograph (MEYE-kroh-graf)**
A kind of visual. A micrograph is a photograph taken with the help of a microscope. We use microscopes to see small things up close.

**minerals (MIN-uh-ruhlz)**
The substances that make up rocks.

Minerals are solid and come from nature. There are over 3,000 minerals. Copper is an example of a mineral.

**observe (uhb-ZERV)**
Step 4 of the scientific method. To observe is to watch something in order to learn about it. When you do an experiment, you write down what you observe.

**orbit (OR-buht)**
**1.** *(Verb)* to move around another object in space. Earth orbits the sun.
**2.** *(Noun)* the path an object takes as it moves in space. Earth's orbit is oval.

**outer core (OWT-uhr kor)**
Third layer of the Earth. It is made of liquid metal.

**outer planets (OWT-uhr PLAN-uhts)**
The four planets that are farthest away from the sun. They are made up mostly of gases and are very cold. Jupiter, Saturn, Uranus, and Neptune are the outer planets.

**oval (OH-vuhl)**
Shaped like an egg. Orbits are oval.

**particles (PAR-tuh-kuhlz)**
Very small pieces.

**poisonous (POY-zuh-nus)**
Containing substances that harm or kill people.

**preview (PREE-vyoo)**
A reading strategy. To preview a text, look at the headings, pictures, and captions before you start reading. This will help focus your attention.

**properties (PROP-uhr-teez)**
Traits, or qualities. Each mineral has different properties. A diamond, for example, is clear and very hard.

**reread** (ree-reed)
A reading strategy. To reread is to read again. Reread difficult parts of the text to understand them better.

**scientific method**
(seye-uhn-TIF-ik METH-uhd)
The way scientists find out about the world. There are 5 steps in the scientific method: **1.** Ask questions, **2.** Make a hypothesis, **3.** Test the hypothesis, **4.** Observe, and **5.** Draw conclusions.

**sedimentary** (sed-uh-MEN-tuh-ree)
The kind of rock that forms when layers of sand, mud, and tiny pieces of rock join together and become hard over thousands of years.

**solar system** (SOH-luhr SIS-tuhm)
A group of objects that orbit a star. In our solar system, eight planets, asteroids, and comets orbit a star called the sun.

**spiral** (SPEYE-ruhl)
Round; one shape that a galaxy can be.

**surface** (SUHR-fis)
The outside or top part of something.

**telescope** (TEL-uh-skohp)
A tool that lets scientists see planets, stars, and galaxies in space.

**test the hypothesis**
(test thuh heye-PAH-thuh-suhs)
Step 3 of the scientific method. You test the hypothesis to see if it is correct. Doing an experiment is how a scientist tests his or her hypothesis.

**tools** (toolz)
What scientists use to observe and measure things. A thermometer, a ruler, and a microscope are all tools.

**trillion** (TRIL-yuhn)
The number 1,000,000,000,000. A trillion is a million million.

**universe** (YOO-nuh-vers)
Everything in space, including planets, stars, and galaxies.

**visualize** (VIZH-oo-uh-leyez)
A reading strategy. To visualize is to picture things in your mind. As you read, visualize the ideas in the text.

**volcano** (vol-KAY-noh)
A hole in the Earth's crust through which hot liquid rock comes above ground. When a volcano erupts, hot liquid rock bursts out with great force.

**weathering** (WETH-uhr-ing)
The breaking down of rock into small pieces. Water, wind, air, plants, and animals can cause weathering.

# Index

# Credits